MW01595503

JOSUA

THANK YOU FOR YOUR
FAITHFULNESS TO HIM?

MIKE

Michael J Schultz

12-20-12

1

God, the Mosquito, and Man

God, the Mosquito, and Man

The true story of a man trying to know God while trying to understand the meaning of His purpose as he watches his two sons deal with cystic fibrosis.

Michael J. Schultz

God, the Mosquito, and Man

God, the Mosquito, and Man

Chapter One

God: All powerful, all knowing, all present. What can be written about Him that has not already been discussed or talked about over the ages? Discussions that have taken place over campfires to pass away the time while trying to keep warm, inside foxholes when death might be eminent, inside bar rooms under the influence of too much alcohol to have any reasonable amount of rational understanding, or while lying on your death bed waiting for the last breath, at which time you will know the answers to this age old question. Some say He does not exist; others are willing to lose their lives for Him! Some have made fortunes because of Him, some have lost their fortunes because of Him and yet others have given their fortunes to Him. There have been more discussions about Him, more books about Him and more songs about

Him than any other. Yet man still questions if He exist and if He does, why does He tolerate all of the tragedy, the sorrow, the pain, and suffering if He is such a loving God?

The Mosquito: An annoying little creature that seems to have been put here on earth with the sole purpose of interfering with our relationship between man and his God. You might say they are a lot like demons and man questions the very purpose of their existence. They have the ability to influence the friends of man in many ways. They are known to carry major diseases but when they infect the friend of man, that infected man can be used by them to influence man in his spirit and relationship with his God while inducing suffering in his physical body. They are led by the King of Mosquitos, Lucifer, Satan, or more commonly known as the Devil. Although He opposes everything that God stands for he is not the opposite of God but the opposite of Michael and Gabriel, the obedient arc angles.

The King Mosquito also shared in that high and trusted position at one time. His existence, like God is also questioned by man.

Man: Created by God to have fellowship with Him, but was robbed of that fellowship by the King Mosquito. Man is always questioning, sometimes cursing, sometimes praying but is always in turmoil over his own existence. It has been going on since the creation of man and will continue until the very end that God has ordained that it shall cease and the fellowship be restored.

Chapter Two

Friend of Man: Mosquitoes, mosquitoes, it is so unbearably hot today and with the humidity and these mosquitos I am about to go insane! They seem to be sucking the very life blood out of me, constantly buzzing and always stalking me for a free meal. If I could see their face and look into their eyes I would bet there is a determined, death defying and almost hypnotic trance that no amount of reasoning on my behalf would make them go away so I could have some peace. Why do you suppose that God even created such a thing? Like we believe in God!

Man: Good question. I have often thought about that myself and like you, I have often wondered why they are even in existence. However to address your other statement, you and I have been friends for years and neither one of us have ever said that we believe in God. Oh, we have made casual references and told jokes about Him, even used His name repeatedly but usually in a curse word that spews out of our mouth from anger or habit. I am with you though, if I could eliminate all of the mosquitoes from the face of the earth, I am sure I would be considered one of the greatest men to have ever lived.

Friend of Man: Well if there were a God, I would tell Him to His face that he sure wasted a lot of time and energy creating something as worthless as the mosquito. Think about it, you cannot think of any reason for their existence. They do not pollinate anything and there certainly is no beauty in their form. When was the last time anyone ever looked at a mosquito and said, oh what a beautiful mosquito? Instead when one lands on us we instinctively swat it. Even the people for the ethical treatment of animals when they are protesting at some rally will swat the mosquito without a second thought. I have never met one person who likes the mosquito. The only things that seem to benefit from them are the mosquito hawk and some birds and bats. They wake us up in the middle of the night with t heir constant humming and we know that if there is one in the room he will not be satisfied or quiet until he has left his mark on our body. Have you ever watched one when he lands on you? He immediately takes a four legged stance, the front two legs higher in the air, I guess for traction. He then slowly bows his head like he is getting ready to ask God to bless the meal he is about to receive. As he inserts his proboscis or whatever you call it into your flesh you can watch his stomach turn from a brownish black to a reddish purple. When he is finished he leaves a little raised red mark that will itch and aggravate you the rest of the night reminding you that he has been in touch. Meanwhile the little varmint flies happily away as his wings hum out some happy melody with his belly full of our life giving blood. In addition, God only knows if he has just infected us with some incurable disease. Oh, I wish you did have the power to eliminate all of them. I would be one of the first to bow down at your feet and say, you are God!

Man: Well if I were God that would be one of my first priorities, to torture and eradicate every last one of them. However the more I think about it, there might be more pressing matters that would need my attention, if I were God.

Friend of Man: Like what?

Man: Well I could say the usual things like world peace, eradicating hunger, removing the hurt and pain from everyone and so on. You know sort of like the hippies back in the sixties only without the drugs. That is probably what most people would do if they were God. However, I think the thing that would make me the happiest; after all if I am God then I can choose the thing that would make me the happiest.

Friend of Man: And what would that be?

Man: If I were God, the thing that would please me the most would be for everyone to know me and me to know them. Just think of it, no strangers and everyone would be friends and family. Then after that there would be no hunger, war, pain, probably no sickness, and maybe, just maybe even no death.

Friend of Man: Man, you are really getting out there. You are starting to sound like a Marxist. The next thing you will be telling me is that you are getting ready to sell all your goods, give the proceeds to the poor and retreat to some faraway mountaintop and live off the land like an old hermit, and wait for the end of time. Well I have news for you, there are mosquitoes there also. I have known you since the eighth grade and you are ruthless in business. You work, work, work, and having amassed a small fortune, you are trying to tell me that you would like everyone to be friends and family. I think if you were God you would keep everything to yourself and allocate a little to us ordinary mortals, sort of like what is going on in this present time. That is what I think! For that is the same thing that the so called godly are trying to convince us of now. Ouch, another mosquito just bit me!

Man: Well you asked me and I answered what I would like if I were God. I would like to have everyone like me, not for what I could do for them but for who I am. For if I were God, supposedly I would be perfect and not need or crave anything, so the only thing I would want would be the fellowship of friends and family. For what good would it be to have everything and not be able to share it with anyone? You say I have made a small fortune, and say I am ruthless. Well my old friend, you are no pauper. Your fortune surpasses mine many times over. Why do we work so hard? I will tell you. We do it so that we can support our families and maybe help our friends. In addition, we are afraid that we will not have enough money to accomplish that and everyone will see us as an insignificant person. For we all want to be looked up to and be respected and maybe even worshiped

Friend of Man: And here I thought you quit talking drugs. The next thing I know I will turn the TV on and there you will be, big hair and all, asking for money, all in the name of God.

Man: You know better than that. We were just having a conversation about God and mosquitos and now it has led to this. You know that I know absolutely nothing about God. Unlike you who as a young child attended church regularly. Maybe you should be telling me more about God even though you have not attended in years. At least you know something. I know absolutely nothing. In addition, before you can ask a question about something you have to know something about the topic that you are questioning. The only thing I remember being taught as a child is my grandmother giving me a dollar to memorize the twenty third psalm. My theory has always been, if there is a God, He must have created me, and if He does not like the way I am He can change me. I will see you later.

Friend of Man: You have lost your mind. Probably from being bitten by too many mosquitos.

God: Make a note of that conversation!

Chapter Three

Friend of Man: Let's go down to that café by the beach, have a coffee, and continue our conversation we had last week. Call me back when you get this message.

Man: Sounds good to me, at least with the ocean breeze blowing it will keep the mosquitoes away. See you around seven.

Friend of Man: I hope you are not upset with me about the other day. A few things have been on my mind since our last conversation. Mainly, when you made the reference that I had not been to church in years I detected a bit of sarcasm. I thought I would just let you know some of the reasons why I do not attend now and have no intentions of attending anytime soon.

Man: Go on.

Friend of Man: Well, without reveling any family secrets, let us just say that my mother used to tell me that if I did not change my ways that I was heading to hell. But as I looked around and saw the way that her and her friends lived and I observed how they were no more happy or content than I was I saw no reason to pursue it any further. As I got older and more inquisitive, I concluded that if I was going to hell they would be there to greet me upon my arrival.

Man: Well friend of mine, I remember spending many a night at your house when we were young and you getting down on your knees and praying before we went to bed. This is how I knew you were attending some kind of church.

Friend of Man: After I went to college and studied psychology and science, I made up my own mind that the conception of God was a bunch of nonsense and I was far too intelligent to fall for that line. If I ever wanted to own anything and have any peace and enjoy my life then it was going to be entirely up to me.

Man: Do you have any peace now?

Friend of Man: Do you?

Man: I have some peace knowing that I am financially successful. However, sometimes when I am all alone at night there seems to be a hollow emptiness that I cannot describe.

Friend of Man: Financial peace is a good thing; it is a lot better than being poor. If you are alone at night why don't you go out and get you a girlfriend?

Man: You know that I am married and have two kids. Besides I love my wife. Also if I were caught whatever financial peace I have presently would disappear immediately. The loneliness that I am talking about is not physical and I do not even know if it is explainable. It is like a vast emptiness surrounded by confusion, always calling out to be filled or clarified in some kind of way that would make sense. Do you understand what I am saying?

Friend of Man: Sort of, but I think everyone feels that way.

Man: Well if everyone feels that way, I will ask you a question. Where did that feeling come from?

Friend of Man: Who knows! Maybe the whole world is guilty of something and we are all paying the price by not having any peace. I have no answer for those kinds of questions. I told you I try to make my own peace by being secure enough financially and enjoy as many things as I can while I am still healthy. I try not to worry about the things that you are discussing now for I do not think there are any answers to the questions you are asking. Maybe when we die we will know the answers and then again maybe not. If you keep dwelling on those questions, what little peace you have now will become a full-fledged war. I highly recommend that you start dwelling on something else.

Man: You might be right.

Friend of Man: I did not say I was right. I am simply saying that everybody has the same questions as you. There is no definitive answer and I highly recommend that you put it out of your mind before you go mad, for you are starting to worry me.

Man: I think I am going to call my brother. I have not talked to him in a while. The last time I did he said that he had something important that he wanted to share with me and he thought I would be interested in what he had to say. He said something about a life changing event.

Friend of Man: At least you are lucky enough to have a good relationship with your brother. My brother and I barely speak.

Man: Well it is getting late, I will get the coffee and you can leave the tip.

Friend of Man: Sounds good to me. I always enjoy talking to you, for at the very least you make me think. Just think these last two conversations both came about by the annoying mosquito. May he be cursed forever.

Chapter Four

Brother of Man: I am glad you came by. How is Joy of Man?

Man: She is fine.

Brother of Man: And the Pride of Man?

Man: They are both doing well, one is three and the other one just had his first birthday. They are the very core of my existence. I do not know what I would do if anything ever happened to them.

Brother of Man: Well that is good news. How about you, how are you doing? You look a little stressed out, as if you have something on your mind.

Man: Probably so, I am having a hard time sleeping. I don't know why, I never had that problem before. However; I must say you look ten years younger. I cannot recall you ever looking any better. I do not know what you are doing, but keep it up, it is working.

Brother of Man: I can actually say that I have never been happier. I will tell you more about it over dinner; I made reservations at that German restaurant that you like so well. We can sit out by the pond and watch the geese swim and enjoy the outdoors while we talk.

Man: Sounds good to me for I am starving. I hope the mosquitoes don't bother us.

Brother of Man: How was your schnitzel dinner?

Man: The best I have had since I was stationed in Germany over ten years ago. That is why I love this place. It brings back good memories of the time when my life seemed to be more satisfying and a little more intriguing, not knowing what the future was holding for me. Come to think about it is a lot like the present time for I seemed to be a little confused about what the future holds now, only in a different way.

Brother of Man: There is something I need to tell you. I do not want to be bogged down by telling stories about our past. We both have some interesting stories that we have shared with each other many times before. What I want to talk about is something that is happening now and in the future.

Man: Good, because Friend of Man and I have been engaged in some deep conversations that I am certain are the reasons for me not sleeping well. I hope this is not too heavy as I don't know if I can handle any more stress at this time.

Brother of Man: I don't know where to start so I am just going to jump in the deep end and tell you, I met God!

Man: Oh really! How is he doing?

Brother of Man: I will ignore that, but I want you to meet Him also.

Man: Well why didn't you invite Him to dinner? Maybe we could have talked Him into paying the bill!

Brother of Man: I know you think I have lost my mind, but I can assure you that I have not. This is all new to me and I cannot answer all of your questions, however I can say one thing positively and that is I have met God. I cannot tell you how peaceful I have felt in the last few weeks since my encounter with Him. You said you are not sleeping at night, it is probably the same reason I wasn't either. Let me take a guess. You are trying to find peace and the understanding of life. You are looking around and you don't see any peace and nobody seems to care or understand what you are going through. However there is one who understands and his name is Jesus Christ. There I said it!

Man: Yes you did!

Brother of Man: Yes I did!

Man: Wow!

Brother of Man: That was easier than I thought it would be. I thought that I would stutter and stammer looking for some eloquent words to present Him to you. But I just spit it out without even thinking of how I was presenting Him to you. I am so relieved that I have finally mustered the courage to tell you. Really I do not know where that courage came from. I am not like you for you will speak to anybody on any subject in any place even if you are one hundred percent wrong, I am not that way.

Man: Tell me, how did this all come about?

Brother of Man: While I was talking with this person at work, he asked me if I knew Jesus Christ. I said only an idiot would never have heard of him. He said, I am not asking you if you heard of Him I am asking you if you know Him. I said how could I know someone who has been dead for two thousand years? He said, He is not dead He is alive and if you want to know Him, all you have to do is ask Him in your heart. Then he asked me would you like to do that? I do not know what happened except that I had this powerful feeling that I have never experienced before and without any hesitation I said yes. Therefore I did!

Man: Then what?

Brother of Man: I can only tell you that this warm, strange feeling came over me. I could not understand it so I asked the person at work what was happening to me. He said the Holy Spirit had joined my spirit and that now I was joined to God. I asked, how can this be? I have not done anything for God. He said, that is the great thing about Jesus Christ, He died on the cross for us so we could be united with God and we do not have to do anything. At first I thought it was just too simple but the more I thought about it the more sense that it made. I am new at this but I can tell you that the feeling still has not receded. I sleep like a newborn baby, and everything I behold now seems to have a new look to it.

Man: Have you noticed that large swarm of mosquitoes hovering above us? They are making so much noise that I can hardly hear what you are saying.

Brother of Man: I am not paying any attention to them, for I want to continue on this subject and I know that God wants me to also. Therefore, I am praying under my breath that he holds them back from us so we can continue with our discussion.

Man: I hope he holds them back so they don't bite us!

Brother of Man: Back to our subject. You say you are not sleeping, and are confused and confounded by the emptiness that is within you, I cannot explain it but I can swear to you that the answers you are looking for are in God. Neither one of us were taught anything about God, absolutely nothing. Our parents are good hardworking people but there was never any teaching or talking about Jesus Christ. Even right now I could not even begin to explain anything about Him or show you how to find him in a book, even the Bible. I can only tell you what happened to me and I want that for you! I am telling you that what I experienced is as real as the chair you are sitting on. Would you like to have that experience and ask Jesus in your life right now? It could very well be the most important decision you have ever made or ever will make.

Man: I am thinking, please give me a moment. It seems my mind is racing a hundred miles an hour. I am like you, I know absolutely nothing about this subject, and I must say I see something in you that makes me very envious. I do feel some kind of unexplainable tugging on me as I listen to what you have to say. If God has done that for you then I want the same thing for me. What do I have to do?

Brother of Man: Just in your own words, ask him into your life. Nothing fancy, do not try to be overly eloquent in your speech, just be open and ask him. OK? Here, let me hold your hand.

Man: OK.

Brother of Man: It has been fifteen minutes since you said anything, are you OK?

Man: Wow! You will not believe what just happened.

Brother of Man: What?

Man: The moment I started to ask Jesus in my life, I saw a bright light that was constantly getting brighter and brighter. But as the light became ever increasingly brighter the mosquitoes that were above us increased in number and kept getting closer and closer to us and their sound was like the sound that the space shuttle makes at lift off. However, and this is really strange, as the light became brighter, they vanished instantly. Even now when I look up, I do not see any of them. Don't you think that is strange?

Brother of Man: Yes, but did you ask Him into your life?

Man: Yes, at least I think so.

Brother of Man: What do you mean you think so? Either you did or you did not.

Man: At the very moment that I was preparing to ask Him, and I was going to ask Him, is when I saw that incredible light. The next thing I remember is you saying that I had not said anything in fifteen minutes. Do you think I should do it again?

Brother of Man: I don't know; this is the first time I have ever done this. How do you feel? I do not want to blow this and get everything all messed up. Maybe you should do it again.

Man: Maybe you are right, but this is nothing like what happened to you.

Brother of Man: No, I did not see any light or hear the roar of mosquitoes; maybe it is different for different people.

Man: Maybe, but let me do it again just in case. Lord Jesus please come into my life and take control.

Brother of Man: Oh, it took the first time!

Man: How do you know?

Brother of Man: Because you just called Him Lord. If it did not take the first time, you would never have called Jesus Lord. It took the first time, I promise you. How do you feel now?

Man: I can still see that light, I know something's happened, but I can't explain it but this is the first time in years my mind is not racing in the background. I am totally concentrating on our conversation and yet I can see that light. Maybe you are right.

Brother of Man: What do you mean?

Man: Maybe everyone has a different experience.

Brother of Man: If it is, I hope God agrees with us. For there have been a lot of people that have done this before us. The more I think about it, it would have to be different for everyone to make it a personal experience, for every individual is different, so his or her meeting God would also be different. Different, but unique.

Man: I think you are right. I do feel different. Something tells me though, that we have just started a new journey that is going to be quite simple yet indescribably complex. I cannot wait to tell Friend of Man about this.

Brother of Man: I thank that is what we are supposed to do.

Man: What is that?

Brother of Man: Tell other people.

Chapter Five

Friend of Man: You what?

Man: I found God.

Friend of Man: You found Him, really, where was He hiding, under a rock or maybe in a cave? Oh, I know, you met Him in a bar and He was disguised as a young woman and later that night she made you cry out Oh God! Was that your religious experience? Or did you hit the lottery and say; thank you Jesus now all my problems are over and I can live happily ever after. Hallelujah! Which one did you meet? The one that the Muslims pray to, the one that the Jews prayed to, or maybe the one that the Mayans carved on the walls of caves thousands of years ago? Or maybe it is the one the Native Americans encountered while they were starving and being led off their land by the Christians. Did you meet the Sun God, the Moon God or the God of the stars like Leo,

Aquarius, Virgo, or one of the others? Maybe you met the God that dwells in the jungles of Africa. I can just see you now; celebrating Kwanzaa! How about the one that the Haitians use, maybe you can throw some chicken bones in a pot, stir them up, and start casting spells on people. What was His name, Buddha, Mohammed, Jehovah, or maybe his name was Elvis. A lot of people worship him.

Man: Well uh….

Friend of Man: I can tell you now; a leopard does not change his spots. You are a leopard, lying on the branch of a big tree and patiently waiting for a golden opportunity to come walking by so you can fill that craving inside of you that is always crying to be filled. I know, for I am the same way. However, with you if you do not get off this nonsense, the role will be reversed. You will become the prey rather than the predator. As for myself I am not ready to be eaten alive. You told me last week that you knew nothing about God. Those were your exact words. Now you come to me and tell me that you met Him and you would like me to meet Him also. I will quote your words from last week. You said before you could discuss anything about a topic, and that includes God, that you first have to know something about that topic. Well Man, you must have done a lot of studying in the last few days. Now you are proclaiming to be an expert on the matter!

Man: I am by far no expert. I can only tell you what I experienced, not what I know. I do know what I experienced, and that is I met God and His name is Jesus Christ!

Friend of Man: How can you say that? Have you ever studied the writings of Confucius or the Koran or Buddha and compared the differences to the writings in the Bible? You should first go and study all of them so you can at least make some kind of rational opinion before proclaiming that Jesus Christ is God. After you have done that, then come and tell me which one you think is God. I figure that will take at least five years, but before that happens you will be back to your old self.

Man: You are my friend, and I just want you to experience what I did. However, I will take your advice and do a lot of studying but only about Jesus Christ, because I want to know a lot more about Him. He is the one that has changed me, not all those other gods that you are ranting about. I hope to have more answers to your questions someday. By the way what are all those welts on your arms?

Friend of Man: Mosquito bites.

Man: You might want to put something on them; they look like they are becoming infected.

Friend of Man: By the way, how is Joy of Man taking your newfound religion? I do not know her that well but she does not remind me of the type that is going to agree with you. I might be wrong but that is just my own opinion.

Man: She is not very happy about it; she says that she will be watching every move I make. Of course, she has been doing that anyway. However, I can say that my love for her and the Pride of Man seems to have intensified.

Chapter Six

Friend of Man: Are you sure? That is a serious disease.

Man: That is what I hear, I vaguely remember hearing about cystic fibrosis, however I really did not know very much about it. But I have been doing some studying about the disease.

Friend of Man: I can tell you it is not very encouraging. Did you say that both of them were diagnosed with the disease?

Man: Yes.

Friend of Man: God! I am really so sorry. Is there anything I can do?

Man: Pray.

Friend of Man: What is the long-term prognosis?

Man: Life expectancy various between twelve and twenty years old. However the doctors say that they are working on new drugs that possibly could extend their lives beyond that. Now this is strange, while he was explaining the various studies that are going on he said that they are real close to finding a cure, but he said they keep running into a brick wall. He said we know the cure can be obtained and when we find it, we will have the cure for every known disease of man. Then he looked at me and said we will even have the cure for death. I thought that was strange and when I questioned him about it, he said we keep running into the same problem on certain diseases and when we solve this one problem we will solve all major diseases. He was quite confident in this.

Friend of Man: What made you suspect that anything was wrong with the Pride of Man?

Man: Well, Joy of Man has been complaining since they were born that they have an excessive amount of bowel movements, and every time I would pick one up to kiss him I noticed a very salty taste. Almost like tasting salt straight out of a jar. When we were at the doctor's office we happened to casually mentioned that to him. I thought I detected a somber look on the doctor's face when he said bring them in to see me two days from now and let me run a test. When we brought them in they ran what is called a sweat test and that was the major way they confirmed the diagnosis.

Friend of Man: I am sure you got a second opinion, didn't you?

Man: Yes, the doctor even recommended that we should and he gave us the name of a Dr. Kelly from the Baptist Hospital up in Jacksonville who confirmed his diagnosis and he recommended a cystic fibrosis clinic that also confirmed the diagnosis.

Friend of Man: It sounds like you have learned a lot about this disease in a very short period. Just what is cystic fibrosis?

Man: I have been doing a lot of studying, research, and questioning as many people as I can that have any knowledge of this disease. It seems to be basically a disease that thickens the mucus in your body. For instance, your lungs have mucus in then; you know that when you have a cold and you cough it up. With cystic fibrosis, the mucus is so thick that it is hard to expel it. This creates additional problems for if the mucus is not expelled it remains in the cool damp areas of the lungs, which is a perfect environment for other bacteria to grow and flourish on top of the mucus. So they can develop certain kinds of pneumonia that is extremely hard to cure. This can lead to scar tissue and permanent damage to the lungs I did not know that you have mucus glands in other places in your body. One of them is between the pancreas and the stomach. Therefore, as the pancreas produces enzymes to digest food those enzymes have to pass through a mucus gland to enter the stomach to digest the food.

However; the mucus is so thick that very few enzymes reach the stomach to digest the food. Hence, the excessive bowel movements. This is why when you see cystic fibrosis patients they are so thin.

Friend of Man: How do they digest the food then?

Man: The doctors prescribed a pancreas pill that is taken from the stomach, of all things, a pig. I know that sounds strange, but evidently a pig's stomach enzymes are compatible with humans. They must be, because since we started giving them to the Pride of Man before each meal their bowel movements have decreased dramatically.

Friend of Man: That has to cost a lot.

Man: You have no idea. Then to top it off the doctors said that they most likely will end up with diabetes. He did say that in some instances some people live to be in their forties or longer but that is extremely rare.

Friend of Man: I am so, so sorry.

Man: Thank you.

Friend of Man: Well I bet one thing.

Man: What is that?

Friend of Man: I bet you have told your so called God to take a hike since this has happened.

Man: On the contrary! It has not changed my mind about Him one bit even though I have many questions for Him and I plan to bug Him until He answers each and every one of them.

Friend of Man: You are going to have your hands full. Keep me informed and if there is anything I can do, please do not hesitate to call me.

Man: There is only one thing you can do, and that is to pray.

Chapter Seven

Man: Lord, I come before you with many questions. I hope I am not out of line, but I did not know where else to turn. I know I only started believing in you about nine months ago but since I started trusting you, it seems that everything is going wrong so I might as well start asking you some questions and hope that I do not upset you. I really have nowhere else to go, however many of the fellow believers that I associate with tell me that something is wrong with me since the Pride of Man's diagnosis with cystic fibrosis. They tell me that if I have faith they should have been healed by now. So I am now fighting a feeling of rejection and condemnation. Lord, I have grown a little in you and I do want to please you and you also know that I have faith in you. However, I seem to be vastly outnumbered by your fellow believers who constantly tell me that I have no faith or have something in my life that is upsetting you and that is what is keeping the Pride of Man from being healed. I pray that you have not rejected me. The more I study about you in your word the more I do not believe that I have been. However, I do not understand why I am going through what I am going through. I guess what I am asking you for is to at least send me a friend who is a believer in you who can at least encourage me and help me to understand. In addition I would ask for you to draw the Joy of Man unto you.

In your holy name, Man.

Chapter Eight

Great friend of God: It is a pleasure to meet you: I heard that you recently became a believer. Congratulations. I was in the area and thought that I would stop by and introduce myself, and if you're not real busy I will buy you a cup of coffee. Maybe we can talk about our God. I heard you have been having some questions about Him and maybe I can help you find the answers to some of them.

Man: Sure, give me a few moments to finish this.

Great friend of God: Take your time, I am in no hurry. I was thinking about that German restaurant, you know the one where we can sit out under the trees?

Man: Yes, I know it well. It is one of my favorite places.

Great friend of God: Wow! What a beautiful place, this is almost like a park. Look at those big white geese.

Man: I believe those are swans, the geese are the gray and white ones.

Great friend of God: Clearly you can tell I am an old city woman, whatever they are, they are magnificent. Of course everything that God has created is magnificent. Think about it, what a wonderful God we serve! I cannot think of anything that He has created that is not beautiful and does not remind me of Him.

Man: I can.

Great friend of God: What is that?

Man: The mosquito.

Great friend of God: Excuse me, I didn't mean to laugh so hard, but you could have a point. Have you read the New Testament yet?

Man: Yes, and I am about halfway through the Old Testament.

Great friend of God: Do you recall while you were reading Romans 1:20 when it said "the unseen things of God are clearly seen by the seen things?"

Man: Yes, I do recall that and I remember contemplating, what does this mean? I made a mental note to go back to it. This is so new to me that I have probably made a million mental notes. Why are you asking about that particular passage?

Great friend of God: It is a good scripture to understand, for after you understand it you will be able to see God everywhere and it will even help you while you are sharing Him with others.

Man: I am all ears.

Great friend of God: OK let me get started; I hope these types and shadows help to clarify your understanding of the mysteries of God. Let us start with the sun. The sun is a type of the true Son, Jesus Christ. It is always shining somewhere. Even when it is pitch black outside it is just the earth that has turned away. Like on earth, nothing grows without the sun shining on it, in the spirit we cannot grow without the true Son, Jesus Christ shining on us. You see both the sun and the Son have an inextinguishable light that comes from their very core, and that light creates and sustains life, in the natural, the sun, and in the spirit, the Son.

Now let us look at the Moon. The Moon is like the church, it has no light of its own but it reflects the light of the sun. Now when I am talking about the church, I am not talking about the buildings that are on every street corner. I am talking about the body of believers whose faith and trust are in Jesus Christ. That is the true church. I am sure that you have noticed that the Moon goes through various cycles starting with just a small sliver in the sky and culminating with the awe inspiring full Moon that makes believers and unbelievers mesmerized by its beauty.

The stars, they are innumerable, like Abraham's seed. Ever since the beginning of the space program I have been amazed at some of the pictures that are sent back to earth from outer space, especially those from the Hubble telescope. We are discovering millions of galaxies comprised of hundreds of millions of stars. Isn't our God great! The stars as we see them here on earth are like individual Christians, they are reflecting the light of the Son. As you look at them some of them are brighter than others, while some of them seem to blink on and off, which is not uncommon for individual believers. Also, early navigators used them to find their way when they were lost. It is sort of like us being asked for a safe passage from a sea of lost humanity that is desperately seeking a safe voyage in these troubling times.

Let's look at the sea. It covers sixty to seventy percent of the earth. Its depths are mostly uncharted. They say that the pressure on the bottom of the sea is actually what keeps the mountains from collapsing. I do not know if that is true but if it is; it is just another example of how God confirms Romans 1:20. You see the sea is a type of lost humanity because it is always being driven by the prevailing forces and fads of the world. The seas consist of salt water and saltwater will never quench your thirst. The more you ingest of it the sooner it will kill you, it is sort of like sin, the more you partake of it, the more you will want of it and the consequences will lead to sickness or a premature death. Are you following me?

Man: Yes, please go on, I find this very interesting.

Great friend of God: OK. The antidote for too much salt water is what?

Man: I would imagine that it is freshwater.

Great friend of God: You are right; I see you are starting to get the picture of what I am trying to point out. Freshwater is the only antidote. Freshwater boils up out of the earth, and it comes down from heaven in the form of rain. Our Lord says that out of our bowels will flow rivers of living water. When you read the Old Testament, you will always find that the old prophets, whenever they returned to the land of their forefathers were always digging the old wells that had been plugged by their enemies. Our enemy, Lucifer is always trying to plug up the well that flows from within us by enticing us to fall into His trap thru sin because He wants to neutralize us from being an answer to a dry and thirsty world. Man can live a lot longer without food than he can without water. Now think about this, the water from all springs eventually runs into creeks, which flows into rivers, which flow into the sea. Solomon said, all rivers flow into the sea and yet the sea is not full. And so it is with us, as the freshwater that has been poured out upon us, flows from our inner being it eventually runs into the sea of lost humanity. He causes his rain to fall on the just and unjust alike. So you see we have something that everyone is desperately craving on their journey through this dry and parched life. Now remember this, not all rains, come in a soft and soothing manner. Sometimes the rain comes in a cold and freezing form of sleet, sometimes in the form of hail that can do much damage, and sometimes it can take on the form of snow during a blinding blizzard or it can come during destructive hurricanes or tornadoes. Sometimes it can rain so much that the rivers overflow their banks and cause more death and destruction. Therefore, you see there is a price for the water that flows from our very bowels. I will just give you a few more things to contemplate about.

Romans: 1:20 also states that His eternal power and Godhead can also be seen. You can take a fruit tree, or as Jesus said a grain of wheat. They are made up of three parts. You have the root system the stalk and the branches that bear the fruit. Remember we are also made up of three parts, the body, soul, and spirit. The purpose of the root and the stalk is to sustain its life long enough to bring forth the fruit, at which time the stalk dies, the fruit, which contains the seed, falls to the ground and reproduces itself, sometimes hundreds of times over. It is similar to the resurrection. You see, the life, death, and resurrection cycle goes on continually. One dies that many more may spring up into new life. All you have to do is look at the crucifixion of Jesus. They thought they had eliminated him forever but not knowing the plan of God, that by His death on the cross and His burial that He would rise to be the first of many brethren through the resurrection. Then He could send us the Holly Spirit. For now our spirit cries out to His spirit in which we say Abba father. Remember Jesus called the Holy Spirit the Comforter and He will be used many times in that role in your life. In addition you will find as time goes on you will experience many deaths, burials, and resurrections in your own life. However the resurrections will always produce more fruit that is of a more superior quality than you have ever experienced before. Now, remember this there is a time lapse from the time the seed goes into the ground to its sprouting forth into a small stalk that eventually becomes the bearer and manifestation of the new fruit. And during that time lapse that stalk must endure many harsh climates. Keep that in mind.

Romans: 1: 20 also says that man cannot stand before God and say that he knew nothing about Him. It clearly says that they are without excuse. They say when the Pilgrims settled here and started to communicate with some of the Native Americans, that the Native Americans had pretty well everything figured out except they did not know His name. I find that quite amazing.

One more thing I want to share with you now that just entered my mind concerning our discussions about the mosquito. They probably represent demons. I never really thought about it before but as I do now I am quite sure that is what they represent. I will have to think about it a little but I think I am right. Any questions?

Man: At this moment probably a thousand. I will think about all you have just said for this is so clear and plain to me that I am surprised that I have never heard anyone express it before. Thank you for sharing that with me.

Great friend of God: Now remember this one thing; this is really important! These are types and shadows that are made to point us to Him. They are not the real thing; they are a shadow of things to come. Don't start worshiping the shadows or the creature; worship the Creator; the creation points to Him!

Man: I think you are an answer to a prayer I prayed the other day.

Great friend of God: Why do you say that?

Man: As I was praying the other day I asked God for a friend who was also a believer and someone who could possibly help me with some of the questions that I have concerning the Pride of Man. I can honestly say that meeting you is an answer to that prayer. I hope that we can continually meet and talk about God many more times in the future, for I sense in you an understanding of the scriptures that few people have.

Great friend of God: I thank you for that; I also sense in you, a hunger for the truth that is crying out to be filled. I will be praying for you and your family. I had heard about the Pride of Man through a mutual acquaintance and when she told me about the disease of the Pride of Man, and you were a new believer I really felt to get in touch with you for I feel that you need some encouraging. However, after meeting you, I feel that I am the one that is being encouraged along with being blessed. I pray that God unites us as one in Him.

Chapter Nine

Minor friend of God, but still a friend of God: I heard you met with Great friend of God and I am here to warn you to avoid her like the plague.

Man: Why? I really enjoyed talking to her.

Minor friend of God, but still a friend of God: A lot of us and the church do not embrace some of the things that she believes and teaches. Although she is a nice enough person and I think she is a believer, she is always questioning the established doctrine that we are taught to believe.

Man: Two things, who establishes the doctrine and who is doing the teaching of this doctrine?

Minor friend of God, but still a friend of God: The leaders and Elders of the church. Most of these people have gone to college and studied very hard and long to earn their degrees in theology. Also they know what is best for us.

Because of all of the degrees that they have received we should just trust their teachings and not be so untrusting, for they know what is best for us.

Man: I am sure they know a lot more than I do, however as I look at the members of the church I see a great hunger and emptiness. I do not think that we are being fed properly but maybe it is just me. As for myself I want to know a lot more about Jesus Christ, but all I am hearing is the same old teachings over and over again. I understand that the church is called to evangelism; however, when you look around at the members of the church about all you hear from the pulpit is how to be saved and how much you should give. I would like to know a lot more about the Old Testament prophets, and the New Testament promises. Surely, there is more than just being saved and going to heaven when we die. There just has to be.

Minor friend of God, but still a friend of God: Oh there is a lot more; if you work very hard and are very good then sometimes God blesses us in different ways. For instance, maybe if you would become more obedient and not be questioning everything in the church, God would heal the Pride of Man. He only does that for good people who are not rebellious and who are not questioning the established order. You should just believe what the church is teaching and not be questioning everything yourself, for you are starting to sound a lot like Great friend of God.

Man: Then what are the church's teachings that I should believe?

Minor friend of God, but still a friend of God: Be a good person while you are here on earth and you will be prosperous, healthy, and then when you die you will go to heaven. Then you'll be able to walk on streets that are paved with gold and dip your feet into the river of life that runs through it. There is really not much more to it than that.

Man: I have no problem with what you are saying, but I believe that there is a greater purpose to our calling.

Minor friend of God but still a friend of God: Why would you question such a great thing?

Man: I am not saying that is not a great thing. Look what God has revealed to us now and try to imagine what He is going to reveal to us once we arrive in heaven. I do not think we have the capacity to understand what our future will be once we arrive in heaven, for I believe there are unknown galaxies to explore and mysteries that will be revealed to us. So all I am saying is that I believe that the purpose that we are saved has a much higher calling than walking on streets of gold and dipping our feet in a river. There just has to be.

Minor friend of God, but still a friend of God: And what would you think that would be?

Man: To know Him.

God: Well, well, so he wants to know me. Good.

Chapter Ten

Great friend of God: I received a call yesterday from Minor friend of God, but still a friend of God. She seemed to be a little upset, and I had to press her quite a bit to find out what was bothering her. I think I pressed her a little too hard for after a short time she let me know in no uncertain terms how I was corrupting you. I said that it was never my intention to cause you any harm or distress for I saw in you something that I do not see in new believers very often and all I wanted to do was to encourage you. She said that some of the members in the church had great expectations that you would become a leading member of the church and she went on to say that they had checked on your background and your business and found out that you are fairly prosperous. She mentioned that they were going to build a new social hall and hoped that they could convince you to contribute a large donation toward the building of it and in return they would honor you with a large plaque on the wall.

Man: She didn't mention anything like that to me the day before yesterday when we talked but I must tell you that she said that I should avoid you like the plague. When I asked her why, to make it short, she said that you were always questioning the status quo and causing trouble amongst the brethren by doing so. I told her that I was very impressed with you and what you had to say. I also told her I realize I am new in the Lord but I am searching for a deeper understanding of God, but I don't want to be misled.

Great friend of God: I bet I can guess what she had to say when you told her that.

Man: She told me that I should not be questioning things but trust in the leaders of our denomination for they are the ones who possess the high degrees from the universities. I really do respect their degrees; I know they studied very hard to achieve them; however I must say I am not too impressed with their teachings. I do not know why but maybe as time goes on I will understand why they are teaching what they do.

Great friend of God: I knew I could guess, for they are after the highly respectable place in the community rather than knowing and having a deeper personal relationship with our God. But listen to me Man, I do not want to influence or confuse you, I suggest you get before the Lord and do some serious praying to find out what the Lord would have you do. For he said to work out your own salvation with fear and trembling. Make sure that you hear from the Lord pertaining to what He would have you to do in your quest to know Him. Myself, I think He will have you stay there for as long as you are needed there. You will know when it will be time to leave. Meanwhile keep attending and studying and do not be afraid to question what you do not understand or what you do not agree with. In addition you and I need to keep in touch.

Man: I have not made any plans to leave even though I am not very satisfied. How will I know if I am supposed to leave?

Great friend of God: Simple they will ask you to.

Chapter Eleven

Great friend of God: Since I met Joy of Man and Pride of Man I have been praying for you and your family.

Man: Thank you, I know I have a great family. They are the reason for my existence here on earth and I thank my Lord continually for them. We also enjoyed having dinner with you and your husband. I think Joy of Man was listening intensely to our conversations about God. She grew up in a church family but like so many young people she became disheartened but I think she is being drawn back to Him thanks to all the prayers of the saints.

Great friend of God: Yes, she and I were able to talk a little while we were in the ladies room and I can tell you that she is quite impressed with what she sees in you. She said you are a totally different person, to the better I might add. She, like you, questions God about the Pride of Man having cystic fibrosis. I've tried to encourage her by explaining that sometimes some things are extremely hard to comprehend the reason for, but not to give up hope. This is a question that has been going on between man and God since the beginning of time. Myself, I believe it is a question that is going to be answered to each person individually by God. I do not feel that there is going to be one universal answer for everyone. I know that my lower back is starting to bother me more every day and sometimes the pain is so excruciating that it is starting to keep me from sleeping at night. So you see we all have our afflictions in varying degrees. The pain does keep me up a lot at night so while I am up I do a lot of studying in the bible, for I really am not into watching much TV. My suffering is mine alone, yours affects you, the Joy of Man and the Pride of Man. It is all yours and is entirely different. I know you would do anything to rid them of their suffering for it is hard to see the ones we love suffer for no apparent reason.

Man: Yes it is. I know I would gladly change places with them if I were given that opportunity. I suppose it is a lot like what Jesus did on the cross for us. Unconditional love as He took our place so we could be reunited with our Father.

Great friend of God: In a way you have been given that opportunity. For as He gave His life willingly for us, you are given the opportunity, and notice I just didn't say responsibility, but the opportunity to lay your live down for them even though it is a responsibility.

Man: What do you mean?

Great friend of God: Jesus said, to whom much is given much is required. Now most people interpret that as a financial requirement meaning if you have a lot of money then you should be giving a lot of money. In a way there is a measure of truth to that. However; let me explain a little on giving, for giving is one of the centerpieces of our showing God that we take Him seriously.

In the Old Testament, the Israelites brought the offerings of bulls, goats, doves, lambs, perfumes, gold, and various precious gems. These were offered at certain prescribed times for certain feast and they required a sacrifice from the individual's part to show God that he was sincere with his relationship with Him. Now when Jesus came, his teachings on giving became a little clearer because they were not set so rigid in stone. For instance He said to give and it shall be given unto you, good measure, pressed down, shaken together, and running over. He also said to whom much is given, much is required, and He taught us to render unto Caesar what is Caesar's but to render unto God what is God's. Think of the Good Samaritan how he had compassion on the traveling stranger who had been beaten and robbed. The Samaritan carried him to the innkeeper and told him that whatever it took he would pay the price for the stranger's recovery. That is one of the highest forms of giving for we are commanded to have mercy on the down and out. Think of the commandment to help the widow who is a widow indeed. When the Apostle Paul was traveling to far away churches he would take up a collection to give to the members of the church that he was planning on visiting because some of them were in dire straits from being persecuted because of their faith. God has never been impressed by the amount; it is the intent of the heart, just look at the story of the widow's mite. She gave all out of her need. Are you starting to get the picture?

Man: Yes.

Great friend of God: I hope I made it clear and that there will always be people who have needs. When we can help people we are acknowledging to God that we want to be obedient to him, for he loves all his people but he also loves the cheerful giver, for it is clearly stated that he died for everyone. Sometimes when we get overly religious, a term that I despise and I think God does also; he has to remind us of that. We cannot meet everybody's need, especially financially. Many a time God will have us pray for them that their needs might be met. Now when we do that, we have opened up the channel for God Himself to supply their need and we have now become a channel in which He can send blessings through us to them. Now we also can partake in the blessings that are bestowed from God. You see it is not that we give so we can have more, as some TV evangelist say, so we can have a good life with a better home and newer cars, but as we give more we have more, so we can give more. Then when people realize that it is God who supplied their need they will glorify Him and that is what the mature believer wants. Now I am not saying the less you have the more spiritual you are. I am trying to put the emphasis on not letting your possessions get in the way of your relationship with our Lord. We do have a responsibility to pay our bills while living within our own means. The Apostle Paul said work with your hands so you will have something to give to those in need, and then he told other believers if a man will not work do not let him eat. He said to consider the ant and how hard he works, and then he said consider the sparrows who toil not and yet our heavenly father supplies their needs. Jesus said that foxes have holes and the sparrows have nests but he has no place to lay his head. He said to lay not up treasures out earth for they can be stolen or will perish through rust. But then we are commanded to store up for the hard times. You see when you study all of these things they seem to contradict each other, however they really do not. What He is telling us is to hear from Him so we know how to help those that He brings across our path, for you see we are to give to others, not just of our natural possessions but also of everything that we have. In addition sometimes what we have for those in need is an encouraging word, and to give of our time and energy, while always pointing them to their true answer which is Jesus Christ. Now don't be fooled, there are many, many times we are required to reach in our own back pocket and hand out cold hard cash. Otherwise it is like a saying that men have themselves. Put your money where your mouth is. I might add, and then men will see your good works and glorify your Father which is in heaven. Now James said what good is it to tell a man about Jesus and tell him to be comforted and not meet his hunger. So it requires both, time and money! However; in your case, I know at the present time from what you tell me that your finances are intact. However; God has given you an insight into Him that most people do not have, or maybe I should say do not crave, but by Him giving you that I feel that He is requiring of you a service unto him by loving and caring for the Pride of Man. I know it is not going to be easy but by doing so you will also get your heart's desire, which is to know Him. I hope this has helped you in understanding the principles of giving.

Man: I think so, it seems to have boiled down to hearing from the Lord when it comes to giving but if we haven't heard directly from Him then I guess that we should still give as a matter of principle, for we cannot out give our Lord, but I do have a question.

Great friend of God: Feel free to ask anything, for when you ask a question you show your desire to know the truth.

Man: How do you deal with the problem of people that you are trying to help to become more self-sufficient, but instead of becoming independent they start expecting more and more help from you? It seems like rather than helping them you are actually harming them. Do you understand what I am asking?

Great friend of God: Yes, this can be an ongoing problem. I have had to deal with this many times myself and I can tell you how I feel about it based on my interpretations of the scriptures. What you are saying is sometimes you feel that the ones you are trying to help are using you, and nobody wants to feel that way. Is this what is happening?

Man: Yes, I suppose that is my question so how do I deal with it without feeling some resentment?

Great friend of God: Well, I can start out by saying that I am sure our Lord dealt with this same problem in the form of temptations straight from the Devil himself. Because when you think about what you just asked that is the only place where that thought would originate from, the pit of hell. I am not saying this to condemn you or to make you feel bad or to hold you in judgment. It is as I said I had to deal with that same question many times and once I realized the source of where it was coming from I started to get an answer.

Man: I can see that you are right in saying where the thought originated from, and now that I see that, maybe I can answer my own question. Let me know if you think I have this right.

Great friend of God: Please do, for I am not convinced that my own understanding is one hundred percent right.

Man: I am reminded of the time when the disciples asked Jesus how many times they should forgive someone. They asked should we forgive them seven times and he replied no seventy times seven times, which meant that there was no limit on how many times to forgive someone. So part of the answer to my question has to deal with forgiveness on my behalf in feeling that I am being used. I am being used, but not by a man but by God. Then I am reminded when the Lord says his spirit will not always strive with man, so I guess what that means is to help as long as the Lord leads me to and by doing so I am being obedient unto Him, and by being obedient I am the one that will receive the blessing from God. It is sort of like witnessing, as I heard someone say once; "witnessing is sharing Jesus Christ in the power of the Holy Spirit and leaving the results to God".

Great friend of God: I suppose that is what we have the hardest thing doing, is it not?

Man: What is that, witnessing?

Great friend of God: No, leaving the results to God.

Chapter Twelve

Friend of Man: How is your business doing?

Man: You know how businesses are, sometimes you have more than you want and sometimes you don't have enough. Collecting money from people is getting more difficult every year.

Friend of Man: Yes, I know about collecting money from people. It is as if some of the people who owe me money are making a game out of trying to find out how to beat me out of it. But I would think in your case, seeing how you have been so close to God in the last eight years that you would have a special way of collecting.

Man: You mean like telling God to send an angel to break a person's arm because he won't pay me?

Friend of Man: Something like that. You are always telling me how great He is and that I should trust in Him. I do not see where He is doing anything for you or making your life any easier than mine. If He loves you, why are you going through the same things that I am? What is the advantage of so-called trusting in Him? I would think that you Christians would have all of that figured out by now. After all, how long have you had to work it out? What has it been now, two thousand years?

Man: Something like that, give or take a few years.

Friend of Man: Then tell me the advantage of being a Christian.

Man: One of the main advantages for me is getting to know Him more every day and realizing that my sins are forgiven.

Friend of Man: You have no way of proving that. As for myself I just try to be as good as I possibly can and to keep the Ten Commandments.

Man: Are you sure you keep the Ten Commandments?

Friend of Man: Yes, I don't rob or murder anyone; I work hard for my family so they won't have to work this hard.

Man: There is one commandment that seems to make us all guilty, the one that says thou shall not covet.

Friend of Man: What do you mean?

Man: Jesus said if we break one of the commandments, we are guilty of breaking them all. How many times have we seen someone who has a lot more possessions and wealth and not wish that we could be like them? Our neighbors drive up in a new car and we wish it was ours. That is coveting, wanting something that is not ours.

Friend of Man: If I am guilty of that, you are also.

Man: Yes, we are all guilty and there is nothing we can do to rectify that outside of asking Jesus Christ to forgive us. I know that sometimes it seems confusing but the law or

Ten Commandments were given to us by God to show us that we are not capable of pleasing Him by our works. We try so hard but when we look at what we have strived for, we see that it still has not brought us to that measure of perfection that is demanded of us.

Friend of Man: Well my friend, here is the way I see it. I believe it is something like this. God keeps a running record of what we have done, sort of like a balance sheet. On one side He keeps a record of our good deeds and on the other side are our bad deeds.

Man: Let me interrupt you right there. I know exactly what you are going to say. You are going to tell me if we have more good deeds than bad deeds then we will be all right in His eyes. Many people think that, and I must admit I thought that way myself at one time. However, when you study the bible you will find out if that were true there would be no need for Jesus Christ's crucifixion. Let's talk about Cain and Abel.

Friend of Man: Isn't that the story where one of them kills the other one?

Man: Yes, but let me expound on the whole story.

Friend of Man: Go ahead, for I know you are going to anyway.

Man: Yes I am. You see they both wanted to present an offering to God, but consider this. Cain was a tiller of the field, in our day we would call him a farmer and he set out to prepare his offering. The first things he had to do was clear the ground of trees, weeds, and stones. Then he plowed it with a team of oxen, I might add that that was a hard task just in itself. He then planted the seed, another backbreaking chore. You and I both know about this for we both like gardening. Now after the seed was planted he had to keep a continual eye on the young plants. Going down to the river to draw water in a pail and watering each plant individually. Another backbreaking job. Now he has to keep a lookout for pest, insects, and disease. All the time the sun was beating down on him and I am sure the perspiration was running freely as he toiled. He then had to harvest the crops, which consisted of some more hard work. As you can see, it all consisted of a lot of hard backbreaking work. However at the end of his labor he did the right thing and offered to God the very best produce of his field. He tried his very best to please God but his offerings was rejected.

Friend of Man: It does not sound fair to me. I mean he did his very best and I would think God would be well pleased.

Man: That is the problem, he did his very bet. Before I go on to the story of Able I will just ask you who made the seed grow that he planted?

Great friend of God: Well he sure helped it a long; I mean look at all the hard work that he did. You emphasized that a lot. And now he has been rejected for all of his hard work.

Man: No, he wasn't rejected, his offering was rejected. God even told him to not have such a long face and not to be discouraged. He even encouraged him to do better the next time and his offering would be accepted but also warned him that sin was lying at the door and wanting to rule over him, but God told him to rule over it. Now let us go to his brother Abel. You can imagine Abel, lying under the shade of a large tree overlooking his flock of sheep and watching his brother out working in the field. I often wondered what was going through his mind at that time. I can just imagine him thinking, what is my brother doing? I am sure that the two of them had some kind of barter system where they would trade sheep for produce and vice versa. I know that is not in the scripture but I would not be surprised if that was happening. Now maybe over time, Cain became a little resentful with the fact that he was working so hard while his brother was lying in the shade. It is just something to think about. Meanwhile when it comes time for Abel to present his offering to God, he gets up from under the shade tree and casually walks up to his flock, grabs a young perfect lamb, slays it and offers it unto God. God totally accepts his offering while rejecting Cain's hard work.

Friend of Man: It just does not make sense. To me it should be like business, the harder you work the better your reward should be.

Man: Let me just make a comment on that analogy.

Friend of Man: What is that, that people didn't work hard enough and failed?

Man: No many people have worked much harder than you and I and have still failed. Would that be fair if you applied that to the rewards that you would receive from God? Of course not! For with that line of thinking, those who failed would be rejected even though they tried as hard as they could.

Friend of Man: Maybe they just made some stupid mistakes.

Man: You are missing the point concerning the proper offering to God.

Friend of Man: No, I don't think I am. I think that as long as I am trying to do my best that is all He is asking of me. Besides, I do not get the connection between Cain's offering and Abel's.

Man: It is simple. Cain's offering represents our own works; Abel's represents God's work for us; which is Jesus Christ, the true Lamb of God as our only acceptable offering to Him. By the way, your phone is ringing.

Friend of Man: I have to go but let's continue this discussion tomorrow. I think I can show you where you are wrong.

Chapter Thirteen

Man: Is everything OK?

Friend of Man: Yes, a check I received from my customer bounced however I got it straightened out. Sometimes I wonder if it is worth it.

Man: I think at times we all wonder the same thing.

Friend of Man: Let's talk some more about what we were talking about last night.

Man: Do you mean about Cain and Abel?

Friend of Man: No, not exactly but about offerings to God.

Man: I am glad to see that you are starting to acknowledge that He exist, for this is very encouraging.

Friend of Man: That is not what I was saying; I was referring to last night's conversation when you were saying that the only acceptable offering to God was Jesus Christ's crucifixion. What about all the people that have never heard of him?

Man: Currently with the mass media coverage that we have throughout the world there are very few people who have never heard. However I do acknowledge there would be some, especially centuries before we had this coverage. Are those the ones you are asking about?

Friend of Man: Yes, both of them.

Man: That is a very good question, for I have dwelt on that myself.

Friend of Man: You sound like you are stalling, as if you are trying to think of the right answer.

Man: I am.

Friend of Man: I told you last night than I could prove you wrong. It looks like I have, so mark one up for me.

Man: Not yet. Do you remember a few years ago when I was telling you about Romans 1: 20?

Friend of Man: Sort of, wasn't that something about the sun, the moon, the stars and all that other stuff?

Man: Yes, here let me read it for you.

Friend of Man: I suppose there is no stopping you.

Man: You asked the question so let me read this to you. "For the invisible things of Him from the creation of the world are clearly seen, being understood by the things that are made, even his eternal power and Godhead; so that they are without excuse." That makes it very clear that none of us have any excuses.

Friend of Man: Well that all sounds wonderful, especially if everybody has the intelligence to figure that mystery out. But how is that going to apply to say an uneducated person, or how do I put this without offending you, a person with limited mental capacities? For there are a lot of people throughout history that have been born with brain damage, or in the case of that scripture that you were quoting, what if they were born blind? If they can't see, how could they put the picture together that you are referring to? What if they can't hear? Are they going to hell because they never heard the word you are proclaiming about Jesus Christ being the only way to heaven? If they cannot hear then they cannot hear that message so I guess it is off to hell with them. Oh well, too bad for them! I don't know about you but that does not seem fair to me. How about the Muslims? If you went over to the Mideast and started preaching Jesus Christ, He would not be received very well. However; let's just say that you did and you even got one convert. That convert would be killed more than likely by his family and if he were not killed he would at the very least become a cast out and would never be allowed to have any contact with them.

Man: You must be eating too much sugar.

Friend of Man: Why do you say that?

Man: Because, the mosquitoes are all over you.

Friend of Man: I know it and they are literally driving me insane. I am sorry to have to cut our little talk short but I cannot take these mosquitoes any longer tonight. This will give you a little time to try to figure out the answers to my questions. Have a good evening.

Chapter Fourteen

Man: Father, I come to you with more questions. It seems that the longer I know you the more questions I have. You know that I talked with Friend of Man earlier this evening and he was bringing up a lot of questions that I don't know if I have the correct answers to. You also know that in my heart I have wrestled with some of the same questions myself. I would imagine that almost every believer has at one time in his life pondered the same questions. I know you have said in your word that there is nothing new under the sun, so I would imagine that these questions have been going on from the very beginning. However, in your word you said for us to seek and we shall find. Well Lord, you know I have been seeking, yet I still have not found the answers. I am not saying that I am going to quit seeking but I am asking for you to help me by opening the eyes of my understanding. I would like to especially thank you for keeping your hands on the Pride of Man by keeping them healthy.   I ask for their continued grace from you. I also thank you for drawing the Joy of Man unto you and I thank you for the many unearned blessings that you have bestowed upon me and I ask for the continual blessings and fellowship of your spirit. Your word says in Psalms that your thoughts of me are continual and they outnumber the sands of the sea. I know sometimes I forget that when I am down but I ask for you to remind me.

God: Do you still want to know me?

Man: Yes Lord.

Chapter Fifteen

Man: Those are the questions that Friend of Man was trying to discourage me with.

Great friend of God: I hope you did not let that happen.

Man: No I guess I am becoming more like you.

Great friend of God: I don't know if that's good or bad.

Man: What I mean is when I have a question it's starting to make me study and pray and ask people like you who might have some more insight than I do. Those questions rarely deter me; however I would like to have the capability of answering those people who are purposely trying to discourage me by asking those same age old questions. I just hope that I am not trying to find an answer so everyone will put me up on some kind of pedestal because they think I am so brilliant.

Great friend of God: I know what you mean for if we are put up on a pedestal sometimes someone will come by and knock us off of it.

Man: Well said, however if you have any answers to those questions please feel free to share, and I will not put you up on a pedestal.

Great friend of God: Don't get discouraged if someone asks you a question you cannot answer, for let me ask you this question. When we die and face God do you think we are going to be given a paper with a bunch of tests questions on it? Think about it, if there was such a thing, what would be on the test? Would we be tested by the Baptist, the Methodist, the Pentecostals or the Roman Catholic Church?

Man: Probably none of the above.

Great friend of God: Of course not! Who would like to be given a written test prepared by God? Think of where that could lead to. Are we going to walk around heaven for eternity boasting to everybody about our grade? We could be so proud, could we not? That didn't work out too well for Lucifer did it? Nevertheless he is the one that is behind questions like that. If you could answer all the questions that will be presented to you in your lifetime it will not influence your relationship with God, however in converse to that if you could not answer the same questions that does not influence your relationship with God either. Are you starting to understand?

Man: Yes, but you are not telling me not to try to seek for the answers to hard questions, are you?

Great friend of God: On the contrary, we are commanded to study to show ourselves approved. Our God will allow questions like that to come our way and they usually come through our friends to keep us humble. When you read in the scriptures you find the quote, not many mighty or not many wise are called. You see this does not mean that we are all a bunch of idiots, like some might think, but it means that we have come to God knowing our failures and God still accepts us. As the song says "just as I am a without one plea, but that thy grace was shed for me." But I am sure you have read where Jesus said, you have not chosen me, I have chosen you. I think He said that to keep us humble. When you have questions like the ones presented to you, does it make you want to give up and quit? I know you don't! Even if you did know the answer to those questions, sometimes God will allow your mind to go blank and let the one who is asking them to be overtaken by their own deception.

Man: Go on.

Great friend of God: I could answer some of those questions for myself; however some of those will be answered to you personally. Especially those concerning the way people are born.

Man: Do you mean about the Pride of Man having cystic fibrosis question?

Great friend of God: Yes, for I know that is an ongoing concern for you. I can tell you it is an ongoing concern for me also having met the two of them. They are such sweet young men, I ask God myself for an answer also.

Man: You might be right, maybe I want to know the answers to questions I have concerning the Pride of Man. Thank you, I appreciate your concern. However, I know that you are going thru a tremendous physical affliction with your back. Sometimes I can see the pain in your face and I just want to let you know that I am praying for you continually along with the Pride of Man.

Great friend of God: Thank you, for that is what we are called to do.

Man: And what is that?

Great friend of God: Pray for one another. Do you want to know why?

Man: Tell me.

Great friend of God: It is in the book of James. He says "pray one for another that you might be healed." You see by me praying for them rather than myself, although I do pray for myself, but by praying for them I am healed.

Man: That seems to be one of the basic foundations of Christianity, to be more concerned for others than ourselves.

Great friend of God: Myself, I am more convinced of it every day. This is why I tell you not to let foolish questions from unbelievers rob you of your relationship with Jesus. I will talk to you soon. God bless.

Man: You too.

Chapter Sixteen

Great friend of God: I was talking with the Joy of Man the other day and she was telling me that the Pride of Man are now thirteen and fifteen.

Man: Yes they are.

Great friend of God: I must say they look remarkably healthy.

Man: Yes and I would like to thank everyone for their continual prayers for I know the Lord is answering them by keeping them in continual health. I am also blessed to have Joy of Man as my wife. She watches over them and tries to keep them as healthy as she can. If one of them even looks like they are trying to come down with a cold she is on it immediately, for a small cold can lead to serious repercussions for them by leaving irreparable damage to their lungs.

Great friend of God: You are certainly blessed to have her as a wife. I am thinking of the scripture that says; he that has a good wife has a good thing.

Man: It is better than the other one, is it not?

Great friend of God: What other one?

Man: That it is better to dwell on the corner of a rooftop than to live with a cantankerous woman. I believe it is in Psalms.

Great friend of God: I haven't seen you sitting on the roof lately.

Man: No I have not... Thank you very much Lord.

Great friend of God: How are you holding up under this pressure?

Man: I must admit I still have my questions about the reason for their disease, however it does not bother me that much, or maybe it does, but as it goes on year after year sometimes doubt enters in.

But great friend of God: What kind of doubt?

Man: You know, as the years drag by we become sort of stagnant in our belief and forget about all the times that He has blessed us during the times that we felt so close to Him. And when we do not feel close to Him all the time we can become doubtful of our relationship with Him and questioned Him to the point that we even wonder if He is the one we should be worshipping.

Great friend of God: Well that is not uncommon because doubt does exist in the scriptures.

Man: I do not recall reading a scripture that says doubt is a common practice of man unless you are talking about the disciple Thomas.

Great friend of God: No, I am not talking about, doubting Thomas; I am talking about John the Baptist.

Man: John the Baptist, I do not see the connection.

Great friend of God: Jesus said, amongst men there is none greater that was born of woman than John the Baptist. Think about that! No one was ever greater! Here is a man who was not dressed in the common attire of the day, always causing quite a commotion amongst the established quo, especially those in the religious circle of the day, all the while living on locus and honey.

Man: Yes, but does it not also say that he that is least in the kingdom of heaven is greater than he? What does that mean?

Great friend of God: Simple, the kingdom of heaven was not opened up to man until after the resurrection of Jesus.

Man: I wonder why I never thought of that.

Great friend of God: This is the amazing thing about God's word; we can read it over and over and miss so much. That is why it is called our daily bread. It feeds us daily with a meal that we have never partaken of before. Even in our natural life we are always searching for a new experience in fine dining, are we not?

Man: I know that I am, however I still have my standing favorites that I could eat four or five times a week. I understand what you were saying though; you are talking about the milk of the word and the meat of the word.

Great friend of God: Yes. But let us get back to the subject of John the Baptist. We were talking about doubt. I want you to think about John. Think of some of the things that he went through with Jesus. He recognized Him while he was in the womb of his mother Elizabeth. Do you remember that story?

Man: Yes.

Great friend of God: He also preached that there was one coming that was so great that he was not even worthy to untie His shoes. Am I right?

Man: Yes.

Great friend of God: Do you remember anything else about John?

Man: Yes, I remember God telling him that whoever he saw the dove land upon and remain that would be the one he was looking for.

Great friend of God: That is right. Did he see that happen?

Man: Yes he did.

Great friend of God: Absolutely! Now let me put this together and add something to it.

Man: OK, but I still do not see where this is going or how it pertains to doubt.

Great friend of God: Just try to follow me along and I will try to explain it.

Man: I am.

Great friend of God: We have John recognizing Jesus while still in his mother's womb. We have him proclaiming that He was coming, and we have him also recognizing Him when he approached. We have him saying; behold the Lamb of God that takes away the sins of the world. We also have God telling him that whoever he saw the dove landing on and remaining that he would be the one. And we know that John saw that when the dove came and landed on Him after he was baptized. The most important thing is that he recognized him through his spirit when he proclaimed, behold the Lamb of God. Now you would think that anyone with that kind of history would have a faith that would never doubt, wouldn't you?

Man: Yes.

Great friend of God: However, later on after he was arrested and condemned to die, he sent word to the disciples to ask Jesus; are You the one or should we wait for another. That is major doubt. In addition, think of the disciples who also walked with Jesus for over three years. They saw the multitudes fed, the lame walk, and the blind to see. We know that they too also suffered major doubt after the crucifixion. So you see Man, doubt is not uncommon but remember this, we have the Holy Spirit now whereas they did not. The Holy Spirit comforts us when doubt comes upon us for doubt usually comes before the next great faith building experience from God.

Man: I understand now, thank you.

Great friend of God: You are welcome. I am going to hang up and lie down now, my back is hurting so bad that I have a hard time concentrating. God bless.

Man: You too.

Chapter Seventeen

Friend of Man: How do you justify the scriptures that talk about picking up poisonous snakes and they will not harm you?

Man: Do you lie up all night trying to think of scriptures that will discourage me?

Friend of Man: Well if you believe in the literal translation of the bible, you should be able to go out and play in a rattlesnake den and not be harmed if they bite you.

Man: The mosquitoes have been biting you again. However if you would like, I will gladly answer your question. I don't know if you will be able to comprehend the answer as they contain a reasonable amount of understanding of the spiritual interpretation of the scriptures.

Friend of Man: Why don't you try, however try to keep it short.

Man: I will try but I do not think it will be very short. Is that OK?

Friend of Man: Do your best... Please.

Man: There is a literal interpretation of the bible as well as a spiritual one.

Friend of Man: Well how do you know when to separate one from the other? And if God speaks to you and tells you to do something how can you know what to do, for instance like picking up snakes? There is a whole denomination built around people that handle snakes. I would think that you Christians would get together and establish some kind of written order of what to do and what not to do. At least you would all be on the same page. Some of you believe this, and some of you believe that, meanwhile we on the outside are quite amused.

Man: Go ahead and laugh for now, for the day will come when you will not be laughing. I can assure you of that. But let us get back to the literal versus the spiritual interpretation of the scriptures.

Friend of Man: OK, I want to see you try to weasel your way out of this.

Man: It starts out by hearing from God personally.

Friend of Man: Oh now you are talking with God personally, they lock people up in the loony bin for saying that.

Man: You will not give this a break will you? I thought you wanted me to keep this short but you are the one that keeps adding time to it. I do not mind for I am in no big hurry.

Friend of Man: OK, go ahead. I will try to remain quiet; however I do not guarantee it.

Man: As I was saying, there is a literal interpretation of the scripture and a spiritual interpretation also. To keep it short I will use only one example, however if I thought about it I could come up with many more. Let us use one of the Ten Commandments. The one that says honor thy father and mother that things may go well for you. It is called the first commandment with a promise. Now when you interpret that literally it is not difficult to understand. Is it?

Friend of Man: No.

Man: If you interpret that spiritually it means to honor thy father who is in heaven and thy mother who is the church who bore you and gave you life so you could live for your heavenly father. By doing so you are honoring them both.

Friend of Man: Give me another one.

Man: How about mosquitoes? We have talked about them before. In this part of East Florida they are quite common even though they are not mentioned in the bible; they are a reality in our life. In the natural they are the pesky little animal who can drive us nearly insane. In the spiritual they are like demons, thriving off of the blood and torment that they can inflict upon man.

Friend of Man: One more, this time something more Biblical.

Man: How about the Garden of Eden?

Friend of Man: What about it?

Man: I am sure even you know about Eve being tempted by the serpent, or as we call it a snake. And I am also sure you know the correlation that is given to the snake and Lucifer. The snake was cursed by God and told that he would crawl through the dust on his belly forever. The snake would strike the heel of the woman; however the woman would rise up and smash its head. Whenever I think of this scripture I always think of the Joy of Man.

Friend of Man: Why is that?

Man: As you know I live in the country as you do also. It is not uncommon to see a snake. When the Joy of Man, sees a snake, her refined personality changes instantly. She is like me with a mosquito. Something is going to die and soon. I have seen her running barefoot through the pasture with a pair of cut off blue jeans on with a hoe raised in the air and a determined look in her eye. After a minute or two she returns with a look of a general who has just captured a strong fortified city. She will be carrying the decapitated snake in one hand with the hoe casually resting on her shoulder, strolling along slowly with the satisfaction of knowing that she has just been victorious in battle and has obeyed the Lord's command. It is sort of like the comic strip B.C. with the woman and the snake. That part of the interpretation between a woman and a snake is a paraphrased interpretation. The spiritual interpretation is Lucifer, who I like to call the King Mosquito who along with his demons opposes everything that God is trying to do through man. But the woman who rises up and crushes the serpents head is actually the church that was born out of the side of Jesus when the Roman soldiers speared his side. You see this is why Eve was taken from the side of man. It is a foreshadow of we who are the church, whether we are male or female we are the bride of Christ. He is the male we are the female. As we submit ourselves to Him, He overshadows us and He plants His seed in us so that we might conceive new life. That new life within us brings forth the man child that is spoken about in the book of Revelations. I do not want to get on that subject right now, maybe later. You could read some more on the subject in the fifth chapter of Ephesians, where the Apostle Paul writes about a man and a woman and concludes by saying this is a great mystery but I am talking about Christ and the church. Are you following me?

Friend of Man: Yes, I must add you have been doing a lot of studying lately, haven't you?

Man: Yes I guess I have, however it has been Great friend of God who has helped me immensely in understanding the scriptures. Let us continue.

Friend of Man: Please do, for I find this very intriguing for once.

Man: When it comes to hearing from God, there are two different words in the Greek translation in the bible. They are logos and rhema. There has been much said about these two words and sometimes they are very contentious amongst bible scholars to say the least. I will give you my own opinion and let me know if I am making any sense please.

Friend of Man: I will try but a lot of this is Greek to me.

Man: That is what we are going to talk about, the two different Greek words used in the New Testament for the word, word. They are logos and rhema. Logos is the written word of God. If you read it, the logos, without being born again you are reading a book that will always point you to Jesus Christ. This is really all it can do for you unless you are a history buff. After you receive Jesus in your life then His spirit dwells within you the bible starts becoming a whole new book. This is why Jesus said you must be born again. Now rhema is the word that God speaks to you while you are reading the Logos. There have been many sermons preached on this subject, however I will mention just one and that is from the Sermon on the Mount which I am sure that you have heard of before.

Friend of Man: Yes my mother mentioned it when I was a child but I must confess that I don't recall much about it.

Man: I am referring to Jesus saying, "Man shall not live by bread alone but by every word that proceeds from the mouth of God". The word there is rhema. It is that personal word that God speaks to you from His heart to yours. It is that word that gives us life; however you must read the logos and have some understanding of it to receive the rhema. It is akin to reading the Old Testament and never reading the New Testament. When you read the Old Testament you will find all of the prophecies predicting the coming of Jesus Christ, however you will not know Him or understand Him until you read the New Testament. Have you ever read as a child the book of John?

Friend of Man: Seems that I recall my mother telling me to read it. She nicknamed it the gospel of love.

Man: I am glad to see that you are recalling some of the things you learned as a child. This is good, for God has the ability and the willingness to use what is embedded in the recess of our mind to bring us unto Him.

Friend of Man: Sort of like any means necessary?

Man: Yes.

Friend of Man: Even pain and suffering?

Man: Especially that.

Friend of Man: I hope you are wrong.

Man: Me too, but I do not think that I am. I want to get back to the book of John. Maybe we can talk about pain and suffering at another time.

Friend of Man: OK, but I still hope you are wrong about the pain and suffering.

Man: In the sixth chapter of the book of John, Jesus is being confronted by the Pharisees. He tells them that to have life they must eat of His flesh and drink of His blood.

Friend of Man: You mean by being cannibalistic?

Man: That is the exact same response as they had, for He told them that if they did not do that there was no life in them. He also told them that their forefathers ate manna from heaven and are dead, but he that eats of Him, the true bread of God shall live forever.

Friend of Man: I can understand where a saying like that would cause some consternation.

Man: Yes I can see that also. Even His disciples mumbled amongst themselves saying this is a hard saying, who can understand it? Jesus hearing the murmuring asks them does this offend you also? I will paraphrase; Jesus said if this offends you what will you do when you see me ascend up to where I was before. "It is the spirit that quickens; and the flesh profits nothing; the words I speak unto you they are spirit, and they are life." Then he goes on to say that no man can come unto Him unless it was given to him of His father. The bible says that from that time on many of His disciples turned away and walked no more with Him. He turns to the twelve and says, will you leave me also? Simon Peter says, Lord where can we go for you have the words of eternal life. When Jesus says "the words I speak unto you," and Simon Peter says "you have the words of eternal life," both of the times they are the word rhema. When Jesus ask Peter whom do men say that I am and Peter replies Thou are the Christ, Jesus says to

Peter, blessed are you Peter for man has not reveled this to you but God and upon this rock I will build my church and the gates of hell shall not prevail against it. You see the church is built on the rock of hearing God's spoken word to us, the rhema. I do not know how many times that a scripture verse will pop into my head while I am going about my daily business. Other times it might be a hymn that keeps going over and over in my mind, or other times it might be an answer to a question or the answer to a prayer. It is how God speaks to us in a way that makes Him more real to our own being.

Friend of Man: Is that what you mean when you say that you speak to God or God speaks to you?

Man: Sometimes.

Friend of Man: If only sometimes, what about the rest of the times?

Man: Somehow I knew that question was coming.

Friend of Man: Why did God tell you that it was?

Man: No, you and I have been friends since the eighth grade. I just know you have a very intelligent and inquisitive mind. When it comes to hearing from God, it comes to me the way that I described. Some of the time it comes from another person and the rest of the time it comes from a small still voice inside. Yet sometimes the voice of God can be extremely loud.

Friend of Man: When does that happen, the loud voice?

Man: When I ask Him if it is OK to do something that I know deep down inside that I should not be doing. The answer is always a loud NO!

Friend of Man: Have you ever tried to talk Him into changing his mind?

Man: I thought about that once and then I realized that even if He said I could do what He told me not to do I would not be very happy with the end results, for even though God will never pass up an opportunity to teach us something even if it is from our own self inflected rebellion, the consequences of doing it might be extremely harsh.

Friend of Man: I think I understand. I need to lie down now because my feet feel like I am standing on a hot paved parking lot barefooted.

Chapter Eighteen

Man: Lord I come to you with more questions. There are some things that I am having a hard time understanding; nevertheless I know that you are in control but you know what I am going through.

God: Do you still want to know me?

Man: Yes Lord, you know that I do. I am just asking why is it necessary that on top of cystic fibrosis the Pride of Man now has to deal with diabetes. I can see your dealings with me; however I can see no reason to add to their suffering. I do not want to sound like I am complaining but it is just not fair. I know that there are other people in times past and even now that have gone through more than I have. Forgive me if I sound like I am complaining, maybe I am. But in times like this it seems that my faith in you seems to come in question a lot as I struggle trying to contemplate the purpose of another trial. Especially when it seems like my two sons are paying a price for something that they did not deserve to have placed on them for the rest of their lives. Also you know that I do not feel your presence like I used to. I do know that we walk by faith and not by sight or feelings, however sometimes I feel I have been abandoned by you. Lord I just ask that you give me the power and the wisdom to go through this with the Pride of Man. I continue to ask your miraculous healing power for them along with Great friend of God and Friend of Man.

In Jesus name, amen.

Chapter Nineteen

Man: In regard to your question that you just ask, we sing a song that has a line in it that goes, "I owed a debt I could not pay; he paid a debt he did not owe; I needed someone to wash my sins away." Of course it is referring to Jesus Christ.

Friend of Man: I figured that, but what does it have to do with this term grace, that you are always referring to?

Man: The most standard definition of grace is probably unmerited favor.

Friend of Man: That sounds pretty fancy; explain it to me in a way I could understand.

Man: Let us suppose that I loaned you $100,000.

Friend of Man: Well that is not going to happen for I have plenty of money. You might say I am set for the rest of my life.

Man: I am well aware of your financial success. That is why I am using money as an example for everyone can relate to it.

Friend of Man: I like money.

Man: Yes I know.

Friend of Man: I mean I really, really like money.

Man: Careful.

Friend of Man: Why? Everybody likes money, including you.

Man: I will agree, however keep it in its proper place. Remember Jesus said the love of money is the root of all evil and where your treasure is there is where your heart is. Quite a statement but let us return to our subject of grace that you are inquiring about.

Friend of Man: OK, maybe someday we can talk about what the bible says about money.

Man: It has a lot to say about it, that is why I am using it as an example in trying to explain what grace is. As I was saying, suppose I had loaned you $100,000. Being the friends that we are I would trust that you would pay it back within a certain period of time that was agreed upon by the two of us.

Friend of Man: You mean you would hope that I would pay you back.

Man: Trust and hope. Now let us go through a couple of scenarios. First let's just say that you needed more time to pay me back and you came to me requesting the extra time. I agreed because we are friends and I Trust you. OK?

Friend of Man: OK.

Man: Now just because I gave you more time, has the debt been paid?

Friend of Man: No.

Man: That is right; the debt is still in place however you have been granted more time to fulfill your obligation. In the natural world this probably happens a lot, as we both know being in business ourselves. Now secondly, let us suppose, God forbid, that something catastrophic happens to you or your business and there was no way that you could pay me for a very long time, if ever. Let us say you came to me and explained everything and I agreed that I would not take any legal action because we are friends and all that I would ask is that you pay me whenever you could. Would that be fair?

Friend of Man: Yes.

Man: Has the debt been paid?

Friend of Man: No.

Man: Now thirdly, let's say that I came to you and said you know friend of man, you and I have been friends for over 25 years. I love you like a brother and to prove that I forgive the debt you owe me. You do not owe me anything and never will. The debt is completely forgiven and also forgotten, it shall never be mentioned again. Not ever.

Friend of Man: You would do that?

Man: Which one of those three do you think exemplifies grace?

Friend of Man: Of course it would be number three.

Man: Now has the debt been paid?

Friend of Man: If you say so.

Man: Yes, of course it has. Now can you guess where I'm going with this?

Friend of Man: Knowing you, you are going to bring Jesus Christ into this somehow.

Man: I am glad that I have that reputation with you, it is a great honor. Now when I say that the debt is completely forgiven and especially forgotten how do you think you will feel, relieved, grateful, happy, or glad you have a friend like that? Just imagine I will never bring it up again because I have forgotten all about it.

Friend of Man: I would think that I would feel all of the above. However I don't think I could ever forget that you had forgiven that much.

Man: Now to emphasize my point I let us suppose that I do this on a daily basis.

Friend of Man: You do not have that much money.

Man: Let us substitute money for sin. Now let us substitute me, your friend for Jesus Christ, a friend who stays closer than a brother and who loves you more than I do. We owe him a huge debt that we will never be able to pay but He will forgive the debt with only one requirement.

Friend of Man: And what is that requirement?

Man: Just ask Him. You see by asking Him you are also acknowledging that He exists and has the power to forgive the debt that you owe Him. It is really quite simple.

Friend of Man: We have been through this discussion before when you told me about Cain and Abel.

Man: Yes we have and until you ask Him into your heart we will go through this many more times. Are you ready to ask Him in right now?

Friend of Man: I just feel I have to do a lot more to earn his favor.

Man: Speaking of favor, I know you read a lot, have you ever read anything by Mark Twain?

Friend of Man: I remember as a child reading Huckleberry Finn.

Man: Let me give you a quote from Mark Twain.

Friend of Man: I thought you all you quoted was the bible.

Man: I think a mosquito just bit you again. Here, I will quote Mark Twain on his contemplation of Jesus Christ. He is pretty well right on.

Friend of Man: OK go ahead.

Man: He said, "Heaven is by favor and not by merit; if it were by merit, you would stay out and your dog would go in."

Friend of man: Interesting.

Man: It is like I said when I told you the definition of grace.

Friend of Man: And what was that again?

Man: Unmerited favor.

Friend of Man: I have been bitten by three or four mosquitoes in the last ten minutes. Look the welts are starting to swell up and itch. As far as your analogy goes it is very touching however I cannot believe that.

Man: Why not?

Friend of Man: I guess I do not feel that I owe God anything, let alone $100,000 a day as you say.

Man: The $100,000 is just a way of making my point that we owe Him far more than we can possibly pay Him. He wants to cancel that debt and is pleading with you to just ask Him to. When you do that He not only forgives that debt, He also gives you eternal life. Not only has He done all that, He promises to give us all things.

Friend of Man: And what do all things consist of?

Man: All things.

Friend of Man: Come on, you can do better than that.

Man: He gives us Himself and by doing that we have all things. They can consist of many things, not just possessions but also love, peace, wisdom, but the greatest thing is knowing Him. And when we know Him we have all things along with understanding the reason for our very existence. So you see when He forgives that debt we are not just debt free, we have become many times richer than we could have ever imagined.

Friend of Man: I have to contemplate on what you have been telling me. I am leaving now for my feet are literally killing me. Maybe you could ask your God to heal me.

Man: I will, but there is a better way.

Friend of Man: What is that?

Man: You ask him also. As the Apostle Paul always closed out his epistles, Grace to You.

Chapter Twenty

God: Man, wake up and get out of bed for I want to talk to you.

Man: Lord; it is 3:00 AM. Can't you just talk to me in a dream?

God: Get up! I assure you, you will not get any sleep until you do.

Man: Yes Lord.

God: I want you to study the Old Testament.

Man: You know I have read it at least three times and studied some of the old prophets.

God: Do you still want to know me?

Man: Yes Lord, you know that I do.

God: Good, I want you to know me.

Man: But Lord, you are revealed more in the New Testament.

God: When I walked amongst you more than two thousand years ago I pointed to myself in the Old Testament. I want you to find me there.

Man: Where shall I start?

God: I am all over it, find Me!

Man: Yes Lord.

God: Go back to bed now.

Chapter Twenty One

Man: It is amazing as time goes by and our relationship with God grows how He just shows up unexpectedly, speaks to you and then exits the scene leaving you pondering the word that He has just spoken to you.

Great friend of God: What do you mean?

Man: He woke me up the other night at 3:00 AM and tells me to get up because He wants to speak to me. So I get up and He tells me to study the Old Testament if I really want to know Him.

God: Was that all he said?

Man: Outside of telling me to go back to bed that was pretty well it.

Great friend of God: I bet you felt strange and confused, I know that I would.

Man: When I ask him where should I start He said He was all over it and to find Him.

Great friend of God: Have you started looking in the Old Testament for Him yet?

Man: I was looking for Him long before this for I have always wanted to know Him. I know a lot about Him, I know Him through prayer and His word and I Trust Him, however at times it seems I have never met Him. I hope that doesn't sound confusing but I really don't know how to explain it.

Great friend of God: This is good that He is speaking to you, for it shows that He knows in your heart that you really want to know Him and He is telling you where to find Him. Where in the Old Testament have you started to look?

Man: I have already studied Adam and Eve along with Cain and Abel but then I came upon Abraham and Isaac. I must have read their story at least three times before I started seeing Him. The first thing that I noticed was that God changed Abram's name to Abraham but I haven't figured out the reason for that yet.

Great friend of God: Oh, that is easy.

Man: In what way?

Great friend of God: Whenever God changes the nature of someone He gives them a new name, Abram to Abraham, Sari to Sarah, Saul to Paul, Simon to Peter, and then in Revelations when he says He gives them a new name in which no one except he who receives it will know it. So even we ourselves will be given a new name along with a new nature. For the name of someone represents their nature. It is like fathers telling their children to protect the family name because they don't want people to think that they have a bad nature. If you want to do some word study sometimes look up the meanings of some of the Old Testament prophets and especially the names of the twelve tribes of Israel. For instance the name Judah means praise and Judah is the tribe our Lord descended from. I don't want to get on this right now. Do you understand the meaning of the changed name now? After God has changed our nature He gives us a new name.

Man: Yes, the moment that you told me it made perfect sense. I just never put it together.

Great friend of God: You were getting ready to talk about Abraham and Isaac.

Man: Yes, let me know if this makes any sense.

Great friend of God: I am sure that it will for I have started to learn a lot from you lately.

Man: Thank you, coming from my personal teacher I consider that a major compliment.

Great friend of God: Do not thank me for He is the one that has His hand on you because He knows the desire of your heart is to know Him.

Man: You know the story quite well, as I did concerning Abraham. He was told that his seed would become a great nation but when Abraham heard this he questioned God because of Sarah's age. You also know the story of how he went into Hagar, her servant, and produced Ishmael at the urging of Sara herself thinking that would be the one that God had promised him. But a few years later Sarah conceives and brings Isaac into the world. After another few years Sarah tells Abraham to throw out the bond maiden and her son for he shall have no inheritance in the promises of God.

Great friend of God: So far, so good.

Man: Now the next thing we read is God telling Abraham to take Isaac, your only son Isaac, up the mountain and offer him as a burnt offering to Him. Abraham does not hesitate. Now as they ascend the mountain, Abraham places the wood for the offering upon the back of Isaac and Isaac asks, father I see the wood for the burnt offerings but where is the lamb that is to be sacrificed? Abraham replies my son God will provide Himself a lamb for a burnt offering. Now we know the rest of the story, how God stops Abraham from slaying Isaac and how a ram was tangled in a bush and they offered him in Isaacs place. God then promises Abraham that through his seed all nations will be blessed because of his obedience. This is why it says in the New Testament that Abraham believed God and it was imputed to him for righteousness sake.

Great friend of God: I am sure after all these years you have understood what was being shown in that incident was that Jesus would be offered for us.

Man: Yes but I missed one thing that I had never seen until the other night.

Great friend of God: What was that?

Man: When they left the camp to go to offer up Isaac, there were two men and an ass with them, however as they ascended the mountain there were only Abraham and Isaac. The burden of carrying the wood for the offering was placed upon the back of Isaac. It is sort of like Jesus having to carry His own cross to His own crucifixion. In our own lives I see that we also carry our own burdens heading up to a mountain where we are being presented to God as an offering, but our offering is not a literal death to God, but a death to self. We are to present ourselves as a living sacrifice to God.

Great friend of God: I never noticed the part with Isaac carrying the wood himself. As far as that being like our own personal burdens, I think you are exactly right. How do you think it affects you?

Man: I think it relates to my main burden which is the Pride of Man. It is definitely a burden that has been given to me by God for no one would choose this. Everybody seems to have their own burden and by carrying the burden all the way to the top of the mount, God appears and thanks you for your obedience and you become a blessing to many others and you also get to know Him more.

Great friend of God: We all have our own burdens and I think your understanding is very inspiring. Do you have any more places that you can find God in the Old Testament?

Man: He said He was all over it and to find Him, so I would imagine there shall be plenty more. Pray for me that I find more of Him.

Great friend of God: I will do that and you pray for me also. Have a good evening and God bless.

Man: You too.

Chapter Twenty Two

Great friend of God: I was thinking about our conversation a couple nights ago. The one where you said God said to find Him in the Old Testament.

Man: Yes and the more I look the more I find him everywhere in it. I see him in almost every one of the psalms, and all the books of the major and minor prophets. I am trying to find him so I can know him and by doing so receive answers concerning the Pride of Man.

Great friend of God: You keep pressing the fact that you want to know Him. What exactly do you mean?

Man: I mean I want to know Him like I know you or the Joy of Man or the Friend of Man. I want to be able to go to Him and ask Him, what is the purpose of all the sufferings that are so prevalent in the world?

Great friend of God: That is a hard question to find the answer to and rest assured you are not the first one to ask that question. Do you think that question will be answered by God and if so will He then bring you into an all knowing relationship with Him?

Man: I am beginning to believe that understanding the sufferings and knowing Him go hand in hand. But I wonder if the only way to understand the meaning of suffering is to experience it and if it is who would choose it? I know that I wouldn't.

Great friend of God: You could be right. When you read the lives of the disciples after Jesus was crucified, you find that all of them with the exception of John came to a violent death.

Man: Exactly! Just think of the Apostle Paul. Here was a man that studied under the leading Old Testament scholar of his day. A man whose desire was to please God and thought he was doing so by persecuting the believers. You know the story of his conversion and how he met the Lord on the way to Damascus. The very first thing that happened upon his conversion was that he was blinded in his natural eyesight, however he was sent to a man to pray for him that his eyesight would be restored and when it was restored he could see in the natural again and was given a spiritual understanding that no man, as far as I know has ever surpassed.

Great friend of God: Let me insert a comment right here.

Man: Sure, I need all the help I can get.

Great friend of God: The spiritual understanding he received was not given to him instantaneously. We know that he went into seclusion for many years, around fourteen if I remember right, where God had to deal with him and change his whole outlook concerning not only the religious aspect of God but the very purpose of our being placed here on earth.

Man: Yes, however the story of his life after his conversion is very inspiring for he did not go about preaching how to become rich and famous did he?

Great friend of God: Definitely not.

Man: He pretty well started out his ministry by kicking a hornet's nest and turned everything upside down and with the exception of a few who could understand the message that God had given him, everyone, including the established religious people of the day and the government's main officials were against him. Now when those two are against you there is no place you can go and find refuge outside of God.

Great friend of God: You do know that you are not talking about the Old Testament now.

Man: Yes.

Great friend of God: I was just kidding with you. I know you said that God said to find him in the Old Testament and here we are talking about the Apostle Paul from the New Testament.

Man: This is the amazing thing about our God.

Great friend of God: Which one, He is amazing in many ways.

Man: He will tell you to do something and you think you have the course laid out and then He changes the whole direction of the plan that He has just given you. Some people will call that contradictory; however I see it as God being in total control. He could tell you and me to do the exact same thing and lead us each in an entirely different direction to accomplish what He has told us to do and yet the end results would be the same. I guess He keeps us humble that way.

Great friend of God: You are certainly right about that, He does keep us humble and reminds us that in no circumstance will He let us box Him in or put Him in some mold that we have created in the vanity of our minds, regardless of how hard we try. He is the one that is shaping us, we are not shaping Him. Now keep in mind that a large portion of the New Testament are direct quotes from the Old Testament, so even though you are discussing the New Testament you are still studying the Old Testament, for no one had a better understanding of the Old Testament than the Apostle Paul.

Man: I agree with that; however to me the one difference I see is that Paul started his ministry for the Lord with a greater knowledge of the Old Testament than anyone else. So by studying the Apostle Paul's writings you are actually studying the Old Testament. While the rest of the disciples seem to learn from personal experience Paul could go back and tie together the feast, the offerings, and the deeper meanings that were hidden in the old testament that point to Jesus Christ. I don't know if that is right but it is just a personal observation.

Great friend of God: That is a good point for I have been noticing that myself lately.

Man: Think of some of the things he experienced. In 2nd Corinthians he describes some of the things that he went through. Five different times he received thirty nine stripes. By religious law they were allowed to give him forty stripes but by only giving him thirty nine it makes those who are applying the lashes feel like they are compassionate people and ease their own guilty conscience. I would imagine after about ten you wouldn't be able to tell the difference if they gave you thirty nine, forty, or one hundred for that matter. This is why I have a hard time with religious people. He also said three times he was beaten with rods, and three times he was shipwrecked. That is eleven major cataclysmic events that he endured, any of which if placed upon us would leave us discouraged and disheartened.

Great friend of God: Jesus!

Man: He then goes on to say what he called his daily routine, how we was always in peril from robbers, from his own countrymen, in the city, in the wilderness, on the seas, and amongst the false brethren. He then continues on describing how he was often weary, in pain, hungry, thirsty, and how he is fasting often. You would think that someone who is hungry and thirsty would not be fasting very often. But not the Apostle Paul. Then he also said that he was often cold and naked.

Great friend of God: He was a great servant of our Lord.

Man: Yes, he sure was. Then he goes on to say that besides all of that which comes upon him daily, he has the care of all the churches. He then went on to say to keep from getting puffed up, or as we would say becoming egotistical, he was given a thorn in the flesh to keep him humble. He was given this after he was raised up to the third heaven and saw things that he describes as unspeakable words that are not lawful for a man to speak. He also said that he did not know if at that time he was dead or alive. If you read between the lines you can see that he would really like to describe what he saw, however it was strictly prohibited and to keep him from receiving any of the Glory to himself, as a painful reminder to keep his mouth shut, he was given the thorn in the flesh. You might say that is paraphrased by me.

Great friend of God: You do have a way with words, not the most eloquent, but definitely to the point.

Man: He later describes how he would Glory in his infirmities. I suppose that after a few times of maybe getting too close to revealing what he saw and God poking the thorn in the flesh that he realized the faithfulness of God through the pain. This brings me to the same question over and over again.

Great friend of God: What is that?

Man: Is the only way to really know God through pain and suffering?

Great friend of God: Let us continue this discussion at another time for my back is killing me again. Have a good night and God bless.

Man: You too.

Chapter Twenty Three

Man: How are you doing son?

Pride of Man: How did I get in the hospital?

Man: Your Joy of Man called me sobbing saying she could not get you to wake up and would I please come over. When I arrived you were in a diabetic coma, however we did not know that at the time. I called the ambulance and they brought you here and when they tested your sugar it was over seven hundred. They have it down to about four eighty now.

Pride of Man: I do not understand, I try so hard to keep it down and when I tested it last it was about two twenty.

Man: That is what your Joy of Man said. While we were waiting on the ambulance I got looking at your test strips and when I noticed the date on the box, they were over ten years old.

Pride of Man: Oh no, somebody gave me them and I never really checked the date on the box. I knew something was wrong just by the way I was feeling but the readings were in the right range so I thought I was just imagining things. I am so sorry for causing you this burden. I know I am the one with the disease; however I know how much this affects you also. I am so sorry dad.

Man: Son, you have nothing to be sorry about. You have done nothing wrong and I am so proud of you for the way that you handle yourself in this precarious situation. Of course you know that I would change places with you if I could. I love you so much son.

Pride of Man: I know you do dad and I love you also. I really want to thank you for telling me about Jesus when I was young. I cannot explain it to you but these last couple of years He is the one that has kept me going. I can tell you that I feel His presence with me continually.

Man: Again son, I love you so much but I know He loves you more than I do and that is very hard for me to comprehend. It is also very hard for me to understand the reasoning for your unearned suffering for I have struggled with that question since the day you and your brother were diagnosed.

Pride of Man: But dad, have you ever wondered what kind of people we would have become without all of this?

Man: What do you mean?

Pride of Man: I mean what if I were healthy and had become very prosperous. Do you think that I would have been blessed with a wife like my Joy of Man? With the disease that I have I never had to question whether she really loves me. Love is the only thing keeping us together in these trying times. Or if I were healthy do you think that you and I would be sitting here talking about God right now? I doubt it. Also as much as I would like to be healed and healthy if I had my choice, I do not think that I would have ever attained the relationship that I have with Him now. I am not saying that people who are healthy do not have a relationship with our Lord, I am saying that mine and yours also are enhanced by having this affliction along with our relationship with Jesus.

Man: I think that you have really helped me find long sought after answers to questions that I have been searching for for years. The doctor said we can take you home now. Let's go.

Pride of Man: Amen to that. I love you dad.

Man: I love you too son.

Chapter Twenty Four

Man: Great friend of God I would like you to meet Friend of Man. I know you have heard me talk about him a lot over the years and he has heard me talk about you also.

Great friend of God: I am pleased to meet you, Man has told me a lot about you. He also said that some of the questions you have asked him about our Lord have really made him research a lot, for some of the questions have been very tough. I hope he has answered most of your questions.

Friend of Man: Yes he sure has and the ones that he hasn't' don't seem to matter as much to me as they once did. I must say I have been watching him for many a year now and I am more impressed with him every year. I do not know if he told you that I have been recently diagnosed with neuropathy.

Great friend of God: Yes he has and it is the serious kind from what he told me.

Friend of Man: Yes it is.

Great friend of God: I am sorry to hear it.

Friend of Man: By the way Man, where is Pride of Man? I thought you said he was coming also.

Man: He will be here soon. He had to do some breathing exercises first. Look here he is now.

Pride of Man: Hi dad and Friend of Man. Great friend of God it is really good to see you, come over here and give me a big hug. Friend of Man it is good to see you again. How long has it been?

Friend of Man: I don't know, the last time I saw you you were around sixteen. How old are you now?

Pride of Man: Thirty nine.

Friend of Man: Time does fly.

Pride of Man: Speaking of time, do you know what the definition of time is?

Friend of Man: Do you mean like seconds, minutes, hours and years?

Pride of Man: No that is how we measure time.   Time is when the present meets eternity.

Friend of Man: A very interesting concept, I will have to think on that. I must say that you look remarkably healthy. I know two other people with cystic fibrosis and they are extremely thin and frail. You do not look that way, how much do you weigh?

Pride of Man: About one hundred seventy five pounds at the moment, however with this disease if I get sick it is not uncommon to lose thirty pounds in less than a month. So it is always up and down with my weight.

Friend of Man: I have thought about you a lot over the years along with your brother and wondered why such a loving God, as you three describe him would allow you to suffer with such a horrible disease. Look at you three, every one of you are suffering from something. Great friend of God has a back problem, I have watched Man sufferer emotionally while watching the Pride of Man and his brother suffer. Now I have been diagnosed with the very worst kind of neuropathy there is so I guess I am just asking if you three still believe that this God of yours, namely Jesus Christ, is still a God of love?

Great friend of God, Man, and Pride of Man: Yes.

Friend of Man: Well that was unanimous.

Great friend of God: Did you expect anything different?

Friend of Man: I suppose not from you three, but I do not understand how you can be so forgiving to a God that seems to have abandoned you and left you in such misery.

Pride of Man: Let me speak a while for I have something to say about the love of God. I would say that I have experienced as much of his love as anyone in this room.

Friend of Man: Go ahead, if you are anything like your dad there will be no stopping you anyway. I would like to hear how someone who suffers on a daily basis can talk about the love of God.

Pride of Man: Have you ever heard of the three Hebrew children?

Friend of Man: I vaguely remember something about them. Why don't you refresh my memory, I know you are going to anyway.

Pride of Man: The king of Babylon, Nebuchadnezzar, issued an edict that at a certain hour everyone was to bow down and worship the golden god that he had created. Now anyone failing to do this would be punished by being thrown into a fiery furnace. Now this created a problem for the Hebrews who dwelt in the land, for they had a commandment from their God prohibiting such a thing. It is part of the Ten Commandments.

Friend of Man: Yes I am aware of the Ten Commandments, your dad and I had quite a discussion about them years ago.

Pride of Man: Good. Now when the trumpet was blown at the appointed time, Shadrach, Meshach, and Abed-nego refused to bow down. When king Nebuchadnezzar was informed of this he was infuriated and commanded that the three be brought to him immediately. When they were brought to him he tells them he will give them one last chance to bow down at the sound of the next trumpet, and if they did not they would be cast into the fiery furnace immediately. Shadrach, Meshach, and Abed-nego quickly informed him that there God was more than able to deliver them from the fiery furnace, but even if He did not they will not bow down to his false god. Now this statement put king Nebuchadnezzar in such a rage that he commanded the fire to be made seven times hotter and to bind up the three of them and cast them into the fire. Now the fire was so hot that those who threw them into the fire were immediately consumed by the heat. I would just insert here that there is probably a whole teaching on that alone.

Friend of Man: You are your father's son.

Pride of Man: Which one? Do you mean my earthly father or my spiritual father? I have genetically inherited the characteristics of both of them and I am very proud of that fact. Now to continue on with my explanation, when king Nebuchadnezzar looked into the fiery furnace he was astonished when he saw four people in the fire rather than the three, and he asked the question, if we threw three people into the fire why do I see four people and the fourth one looks like the Son of God? So he calls into the fire and tells Shadrach, Meshach, and Abed-nego to come out of the fire. When they came out none of their clothing was burned and neither did they smell like smoke.

Friend of Man: Why are you telling me some child story from the Old Testament? I thought being Christians you would be telling me something from the New Testament.

Pride of Man: You can find him throughout the Old Testament along with the New Testament. For the New Testament is a fulfillment of the Old Testament. The promises that were given in the Old Testament are revealed in the New Testament.

Man: I can attest to that.

Pride of Man: I could tell you about Daniel in the lion's den but the point would be the same with the exception that in Daniel's case the king was rooting for Daniel.

Friend of Man: And what is the point of these stories?

Pride of Man: Simple, that God joins us in our trials.

Friend of Man: But those stories are so long ago, there has not been anything like that recorded in modern times.

Man: Let me respond to that.

Pride of Man: Please do dad, for if I talk too much, especially when I am excited, I lose my breath and it makes me cough.

Friend of Man: Great. Now I have the two of you harping at me. How about you, Great friend of God? Are you next?

Great friend of God: Pride of Man did a good job in getting his point across and I know that whatever Man has to say will be interesting. I am just sitting here listening and learning, however if I feel a need to insert something rest assured I will.

Friend of Man: You three are almost identical.

Great friend of God: Of course, we have the same father.

Pride of Man: Go ahead dad.

Man: You were talking about there has not been anything like that recently. Let me give you a brief history lesson. Do you know the word history is really His-Story?

Friend of Man: Here we go again. Go ahead, sometimes they are even interesting.

Man: I know you know of the apostles that followed Jesus. Eleven of the twelve died violent deaths. Centuries later when Gutenberg invented the printing press the first thing that was printed were copies of the scriptures. The second thing that was printed was Fox's Book of Martyrs. I highly recommend you read it yourself sometimes. There are hundreds of stories concerning the death of the saints and especially a lot of stories of people being burnt at the stake. You have to look past the gory sadistic tales and read how many times that there was a predetermined sign that would be given by the victim if the Lord was present with them in the fire. It happened many times over when people would raise their hands and confirm that the Lord was standing there with them in the midst of the flame. When you study history and the great wars of the past you will see how many times God supernaturally intervened. I am thinking of WWII when Hitler decided to invade Russia during the winter and how God sent one of the worst winter storms ever recorded to stop him. You may not relate to that as the love of God but I am sure most of Europe did. Think of the carnage that would have happened to those people if he had not been stopped. When the communist rule took over in China one of the first things that they did was to shut down the church. Oh, they would let them meet but they could only say certain things and absolutely nothing about Jesus Christ, our savior. They kept the church in constant persecution for decades and even bragged about how they had beaten Christianity and its influences throughout the country. At the end of their tyranny when the church was allowed back, the communist thought there would be such a small number left that they would be harmless. When the true church came out of hiding they outnumbered the previous church for they had been meeting in basements and living rooms, praying to God for his protection and mercy all the while unknown to the communist for decades. The love of God kept them hidden and by doing so the church became stronger than ever. I could go on and on if you want me to. During the holocaust there were six million Jews slaughtered by the Nazis, there was almost double that amount of Christians including twelve hundred priests. Alexander Solzhenitsyn writes about the persecution of the church in his book, The Gulag Archipelago, when he describes the millions of people who were murdered, the millions of people who were sent to prison camps in Siberia, and the millions of people who just disappeared with no record of what happened to them. Most of them were Christians. For the church's true belief cannot be tolerated by any government that has as its main objective complete domination of the people. There are many ways to bring people under this domination; the one that stands out to most people is the use of force. However I will submit to you that one of the most successful ways that has evolved over the centuries is the one of setting up a system of total dependability on government for your substance for survival. You and I have talked a lot about politics and various governments but keep this in mind. Lucifer proclaimed to Jesus that the if He would bow down to him during His temptations in the desert he would give him the power to rule all the kingdoms of the world, for he proclaimed that this power had been given to him by God and he could give the power to any one he chose. The only exception is that you had to worship him, Lucifer himself. All you have to do is look at the leaders of the world to date. It does not matter if they are elected by the people or dictators, it has the same single purpose and that is to keep you from honoring God. Jesus told him it was written that thou shall serve the Lord thy God and Him only. So you see all the suffering and persecution is actually being perpetrated by Lucifer to get you to curse God and to worship him. This is not proclaimed by him, it does not have to be. Why should he take the chance of people finding him out when he knows that if he can get people to curse God they are actually praising and worshipping him. But for those who can discern between the two, the persecution and suffering actually backfires on Lucifer and causes them to cry out unto

God, for sometimes that is the only way that God can get our attention. I probably should say most of the time that is the only way. For nothing makes us cry out unto God like pain, whether it be physical pain as you are starting to encounter with neuropathy, and if it is the kind that you say it is you are going to be in for a hard time yourself. Or whether it is more emotional pain caused by watching those that you love have to suffer. Or it could be the parents of a pretty young girl agonizing over the fact that the girl has become a drug addict and has resorted to prostitution to sustain her habit. Or it could be the same with the young man who turned to violence in a fit of rage and without thinking of the consequences is now serving life in prison without parole. It is still pain not only for him but for those who love him also. I know it seems harsh but this life is very short compared to eternity with Him. So it is the love of God that is manifested thru our trials; for Jesus promised that He would never leave us or forsake us. It is that way with the situation with the Pride of Man. Persecution and suffering makes us all stronger in Him. I am not saying that everyone has to go through it, but for those who are called to it, the love of God sustains them if they let Him.

Friend of Man: I have a hard time understanding the concept of a loving God and now you are telling me that there is a devil. That part I definitely do not believe.

Great friend of God: Well I guess it is my turn now.

Friend of Man: I knew this was coming.

Great friend of God: Good, I hope I don't disappoint you.

Friend of Man: Before you start telling me that there is a devil, I can probably save you the trouble by simply asking the question; if God is all powerful why does He not just do away with him and save us all the aggravation that He seems to enjoy putting us through?

177

Great friend of God: In other words you are asking why he didn't just make us all robots.

Friend of Man: You are trying to accuse me of saying something that I did not say.

Great friend of God: No I am not. The question that you asked can only be that. God wants to be desired by you just as He desires you but He has given you a free choice, otherwise we would be just robots, programmed to do everything perfectly to suit our maker. That is a very important factor that you have to understand.

Friend of Man: Then why did he create a devil?

Great friend of God: Before man was created there were just the angels who served God. They were also given the freedom of choice. Now Lucifer was one of the arc angels along with Gabriel and Michael. When he saw the plan of God start to unfold concerning the creation of man he became very upset.

Friend of Man: About what? I see no reason for that to be something to be concerned about. Angels are supposed to be more powerful than man, we hear stories all the time concerning angels appearing to man and rescuing them from certain situations so it would seem that there would be no desire to be a man if you were an angel.

Great friend of God: Lucifer found out what God's plan for man actually was.

Friend of Man: And what was that?

Great friend of God: That God was going to create man to rule and reign with Him and to have a personal relationship with Him and be given knowledge equal to God Himself. Then he found out that man would judge the angels themselves and along with that he would inherit all things and be given a body which would experience all the senses that the angels themselves desired. In other words man was going to be placed above the angels. This infuriated Lucifer for he was the most beautiful creature in the universe and he thought that this position should be given to him, not to man. This is when pride was found in him and he raises a rebellion in heaven and gathers one third of the angels to follow him and God immediately cast him down to earth along with the rest of the angels that followed him. Just to throw a little fact in, remember there are still two good angels for every fallen one.

Friend of Man: I still do not see the purpose of all of this.

Great friend of God: I know this is complicated and it is even hard for me to explain but let me continue on.

Friend of Man: I did not think you were finished yet but I am curious where you are going with this.

Great friend of God: Let me see if I can explain it. Lucifer's number one enemy is God and seeing as how he knows he cannot defeat Him personally he goes after the thing that God cherishes the most, which is man. After the temptation in the Garden of Eden, Satan was delirious with joy for he thought God would so despise man that He would give up on him completely and bring him and his brother rebellious angels back up to heaven and restore him to that high place that he originally had. However, he missed one thing.

Friend of Man: What was that?

Great friend of God: The love of God for man.

Friend of Man: I still do not get it.

Great friend of God: Let me see if I can finish this up so you can understand. After the fall of man, fellowship between man and God was separated by what we now call sin. This is when God showed his love for man and the plan of redemption and the death of Jesus Christ was then put into effect.

Friend of Man: Keep going.

Great friend of God: To prove to man and Satan how much He loved man He said He would give His own Son's life to redeem the ones He loved so much, which is man. Now listen to this. This is when it gets interesting.

Friend of Man: OK, keep going. I am intrigued by what you are saying.

Great friend of God: He now curses the snake or serpent, who is Satan, and tells him that he would crawl on his belly and eat dust all the days of his life. He, God, says to the woman the snake will bite your heel but you will crush its head. The woman here is the church and the church crushes the head of Satan. Notice that the church is not passive in this manner but it is active. As we walk in the love of God we become more active in defeating Satan, Lucifer, or the devil, whatever name you want to give him. Man and I like to call him the King Mosquito. We are to be on the offense not the defense. The gates of hell shall not prevail against the church. The gates of hell are a permanent fixture and we are to attack them with all our might. Meanwhile Satan knows the plan now has backfired on him and that his days are numbered so he is running around devouring every man that he can. He is one of the most predictable beings there is.

Friend of Man: What do you mean by that?

Great friend of God: He will always over play his hand. If he can make you angry he will try to make you angrier so he can make you violent and do something that would cause you to spend many a year in prison. He thrives off your misery for he knows what his future has in store for him. I could use examples such as lust, money, drugs, alcohol and so on. Anytime he can make you miserable he is more than willing to do so. He will ruin marriages, break apart families, destroy ministries, but mostly he will corrupt politicians. But he always forgets, or maybe I should say the one thing he despises the most is the love of God for man.

Friend of Man: I noticed that you threw politicians in that line. Why?

Great friend of God: It is getting late and that subject could take a while to discuss and explain. Why don't we all meet in a couple of weeks and discuss it. I know Man is quite passionate about it and has a lot to say also.

Friend of Man: Yes, I know he is for we have had a few conversations relating to politics and world affairs. I will be looking forward to our next meeting.

Pride of Man: It is good to see everyone, and remember Friend of Man, I will be praying for you and your disease.

Friend of Man: How can you still pray for me with the disease that you have, yours is a lot more serious and has lasted your whole life. Mine has only been recently diagnosed.

Pride of Man: Simple, it is called the love of God.

Chapter Twenty Five

God: Man, wake up!

Man: Yes Lord.

God: I know it is 3:00 AM; I am going to start waking you up every morning if you do not do what I told you to last time.

Man: What is that the Lord?

God: Find me in the Old Testament.

Man: I have been looking and looking and I thought I had found you in a lot of places.

God: Keep looking! Try the first five books of the Old Testament.

Man: Yes Lord.

Man: Are you still there?

Man: Forgive me Lord. I will look where you said.

Chapter Twenty Six

Great friend of God: So the lord woke you up again at 3:00 AM and told you the same thing?

Man: yes. I told him that I was looking and had found Him in a lot of places but evidently He wants me to find him in some more places. My mind was racing of where to look when He told me to try the first five books of the Old Testament.

Great friend of God: Then what happened?

Man: That was the end of the conversation. Is that the way He communicates with you?

Great friend of God: Sometimes, but then again I am usually up at 3:00 AM with the pain in my back. If He told you to look in the first five books of the Old Testament I would think that He wants you to study the major feast and the tabernacle, something that I have been studying the last two years.

Man: That must be it. I have been studying there also on and off for a while but some of it seems to be a little dry. However after talking to you I think that is where He wants me to look. Let me a read about them again and call you back in a few days.

Great friend of God: OK. God bless.

Man: You too.

Chapter Twenty Seven

Man: I think you were right when you said to study the tabernacle and the three major feasts. Did you ever notice how many chapters refer to the tabernacle compared to creation? There are about two chapters referring to creation and somewhere around fifty referring to the tabernacle. I have heard over one hundred sermons on creation but I cannot recall any on the tabernacle.

Great friend of God: I never thought about it but I think you are right. I know myself I have been studying it relentlessly since we last talked and I think I have a lot to say about what it means for us in this day and age.

Man: Same here, however I do not understand it all but maybe between the two of us we can come to some kind of understanding what God is trying to show us. I know myself I am tired of being awoken at 3:00 AM. I will let you start.

Great friend of God: We are both familiar with the bondage of the children of Israel to Egypt. Of course this is a type and shadow of the bondage we were in before we met Christ. We were subjugated to the terrors of this world and held captive by the cares and desires it had to offer. When Christ comes into our lives God tells Pharaoh who is a type of Lucifer or as we call him the King Mosquito, to let his people go. Now no ruler wants to lose his subjects for his subjects are the ones who sustain his self-inflated ego and pay tribute to him so he can claim them as his own.

Man: I know this is way off the subject but I was thinking of John D. Rockefeller.

Great friend of God: John D. Rockefeller?

Man: Yes, I remember my dad telling me that on his birthday that if you would stand in a long line and pay homage to him when you finally met him he would give you a dime. I remember my dad laughing at the people standing in line and being bitten by mosquitoes, waiting for their new shiny dime. He thought it was quite amusing that people would do that for a lousy dime. I am sorry I didn't mean to get you off track from your line of thought but when you mentioned the word tribute I thought of him.

Great friend of God: That is all right, I can see the connection. John D. Rockefeller tried to buy respect; Pharaoh and Lucifer try to force you to respect them by keeping you in bondage. All three of them do not want to lose their subjects to God Almighty for they know that freedom comes from knowing God and once you have experienced it you will never want to return and submit yourself to them again.

Man: Good point. I was thinking of a scenario where man is falling and falling and out of desperation he cries out to God to catch him. God hearing his desperate plea reaches down and catches him just in time.

For a while the man is extremely grateful and relieved that God would save him from an impact that most certainly would end in his demise. However, after he has recuperated from the fear of falling and he starts trusting in God he then reads that it is a terrible thing to fall into the hands of the living God. For as I see it most men think that they are free and independent and are not subject to any one, however, we are bought with a price, the blood of Jesus Christ and we are not our own anymore. Actually we never were, we just thought we were. We are subjects to Pharaoh or God. So it was with the Israelites being led by God out of the bondage of Pharaoh. They were set free from his oppression of making bricks out of clay and straw to enlarge his kingdom that offered them no hope of a future compared to the freedom that God has to offer which consist of knowing God personally and inheriting all things, including eternal live. While I was studying the tabernacle I could see the pattern that God wants to show those who are redeemed so they can understand what he is trying to show us. For we are now the tabernacle of God, the place that He dwells.

Great friend of God: Yes, that is right. Also he told Moses to make sure that he built it according to the pattern he was shown on the holy mount. Moses was given a detailed pattern of how to construct the tabernacle and it was not to be deviated from in the least bit. Well, let's get started. Feel free to add anything to this conversation as we go on.

Man: I will.

Great friend of God: The tabernacle consisted of three parts; the outer court, the holy place, and the holy of holies. Did you see the correlation relating to man here?

Man: I saw that man also consist of three parts; body, soul, and spirit. Our body is flesh and bones, our soul is who we are. It consists of our emotions and our desires and shows our own individual personality. The fight for man's soul is the battle ground between God and Lucifer. It is the part of us that makes us an eternal being, and the part of us that stands before God in constant judgment. When God breathed into man he became a living soul and he is constantly being tugged on by God who dwells in our spirit or Lucifer who tugs at it from the other way, mainly through our flesh. If we do not yield our soul to God it will be influenced by Lucifer; but the choice is ours for we are created with a free will. Our spirit is the place where God dwells and communes with us. Once we have been born again it has been sealed by God. Lucifer has no claim to your spirit; it is the part of you that God has kept for you and Him so you can have a pure relationship with Him. Lucifer is not God; he does not have the power to create, only to destroy. His only way to influence man is to enter in through the desires of the flesh and when he has accomplished that he will influence your soul. If he can accomplish that he has put up a temporary barrier between you and your relationship with God. That barrier can be and will be broken instantly by God when man calls out to Him. So we are body, soul, and spirit. Is that how you saw the correlation of the Old Testament tabernacle and man?

Great friend of God: Yes, I see that we are seeing the same thing. Let us hope that it continues. The next thing that I saw is that you enter in from the east so you were facing west as you entered the tabernacle. I did not see any meaning in that, did you?

Man: Well the reason that the sun rises in the east is that the earth turns from west to east. Therefore; while walking to arrive at that special place that he is leading us to we are also walking contrary to the way that the world is heading. I hope that makes sense. You are next.

Great friend of God: When you entered the tabernacle you entered through the gate which was on the east side. I see the gate as Jesus proclaiming that He is the only way to enter into God's presence. I think that is self-explanatory. As you prepare to enter in through the gate to meet God the first thing you come into contact with is the brazen altar. Now as with our first experience in coming to God you first have to offer up the proper offering. Our offering is Jesus Christ. The brazen altar is in the outer court. The outer court is a type of our flesh which is part of the tabernacle that God is constructing using us as his dwelling place. The inner court or the holy place is a type of our soul and the holy of holies is our spirit that has been joined to God. Therefore as we enter in we encounter the brazen altar in the outer court; this is where we make our first offering to God, namely Jesus Christ. Old Testament Israel was required to bring an unblemished lamb as a sacrifice for their sins. This was called the Passover feast. The priest would slay the lamb and your sins were forgiven for another year. Now the bible says that the blood of bulls and goats could never take away our sins, they just covered them for a while until the real acceptable offering was made manifest. The Israelites were required to do this until the time of Jesus Christ's death. When Jesus died on the cross he was offered up to God one time and one time only and he proclaimed it is finished. I believe the reason that the altar was made of brass or bronze is the fact that you can shine brass and make it look like gold but it will tarnish immediately. That is the way our body is. It does not matter how hard we try in the flesh it will never be perfect. That is why I call the outer court a type of our body. We can try to look good to others but our body will always let us down, like shiny brass it starts to lose its luster instantly. So when we make our offering at the brazen altar of God it is accepted in the holiest of holies where God dwells in our spirit. He now works from the inside out giving us strength to present our members, which is our body, as a living sacrifice to him. However, this body has been condemned to die and return to dust but we are promised a new body that will never die. This is our great hope.

Man: Yes it is and this is the one thing that sustains us and especially the Pride of Man.

Great friend of God: I would like to make one quick comment. Did you ever think about Passover and how every family was to bring an offering to God? It had to be a mess. Think of the long lines of the Israelites trying to contain the animals that they were going to offer to God. The lines were probably over a mile long, the priest were working overtime slaying animals, the smell of the animal waste was probably nauseating and flies would be everywhere attracted by the vast amounts of blood. Not a pretty picture when you think about it. But it is what God required.

Man: I suppose it is sort of like us when we come to God, not a pretty picture. Do you know what the British say about Christianity?

Great friend of God: No, what do the British say?

Man: It is a bloody religion.

Great friend of God: The next piece of furniture is the brazen laver which is still in the outer court. This represents our baptism and how we are constantly being washed by the water of the word. As you proceeded into the holy place there were three pieces of furniture, the menorah or lamp stand, the table of showbread, and the altar of incense. The holy place is a type of our soul. The only light in the holy place was the lamp stand or menorah and it was to be kept lit continuously. It is the only light in the holy place. Jesus is the light of the world and that light never goes out but it can be obscured. It is sort of like the sun on a cloudy day; you cannot always see it but is always shining.

The next piece of furniture is the table of showbread. There were twelve loaves of bread representing the twelve tribes of Israel. That bread is the bread of life referred to many times by Jesus. For instance; if any man will come to Me I will sup with him; the Lord's prayer where he says give us this day our daily bread, when He broke bread and said at the last supper, this is my body and He also said He was the bread that came down from heaven and whoever partook of it would never die.

Man: Give us that bread.

Great friend of God: Yes but remember this one thing.

Man: What is that?

Great friend of God: It can only be eaten in the holy place.

Man: I wonder why.

Great friend of God: Probably because for it to bring that life changing nature it has to have the light from the lamp stand. Now the final piece of furniture in the holy place was the golden altar of incense. It was located in front of the veil that separates the holy place from the holy of holies. The high priest was to burn incense upon it continually. The aroma represents our prayers to God for we are commanded to pray without ceasing.

Man: When we pray that is a willing choice on our behalf for only believers pray.

Great friend of God: Now let's go into the holy of holies. Inside the holy of holies was the Ark of the Covenant with a lid called the mercy seat. Inside the ark there were three items, a pot of manna that was to remind the children of Israel of how God supernaturally fed them as He led them out of bondage in Egypt, Aarons rod that budded to show them that it was God who had chosen the tribe of Levi as the ones whom he had chosen to be the priesthood that could serve him, and the stones that had the Ten Commandments engraved on them. The mercy seat was set on the top of the arc and had two cherubims that faced each other and God would meet with Aaron the high priest between the two cherubims once a year on the Day of Atonement when Aaron would offer up the offerings for the sins of the people. There was a veil that separated the holy of holies from the holy place and it was to keep sinful man from seeing God and all his Glory, for if he did he would die instantly. This veil was not like a thin curtain but was extremely thick; they say a team of oxen could not pull it apart. When Jesus died on the cross the veil was split down the middle signifying that man now could go straight to God without having to go through a high priest. The blood of Jesus was the final acceptable offering to God. This is why Jesus said it is finished. There is a lot more to be said about the tabernacle and I suppose that as we study it more there will always be something new that enlightens our understanding of God and how He is preparing us to be that dwelling place where He can be seen by a lost world that so desperately needs Him.

Man: As I looked at the three major feasts, the Passover feast, the feast of Pentecost, and the feast of Tabernacle, I saw again the makeup of man; body soul and spirit. For man is now the true tabernacle of God. The Passover is our salvation experience or outer court experience. The feast of Pentecost is the holy place experience, where God's Holy Spirit dwells within us as he leads us to that final feast, the feast of Tabernacles. That is when God's glory comes down and fills the house of God, namely man: for again we are the temple of God now.

Great friend of God: Remember He said that He is not ashamed to call us his brethren and He has made us joint heirs with Him. Think about it, joint heirs!

Man: I think that we have started to understand more about the dealings and purpose of God by studying the tabernacle and the feast. I know there will be a lot more revealed in the future but I hope that the Lord is pleased because I do not want to be woke up at 3:00 AM again.

Chapter Twenty Eight

Friend of Man: I have been looking forward to talking to you about where the world is heading, politically and economically.

Man: We have talked quite a bit in the past but I have never laid out what I see happening in the past, present, or future. I would like to say as Amos the prophet says; I am no prophet, neither am I a prophet's son. I can only speak the things that I see and believe with the help of God's grace.

Great friend of God: I am in so much pain that I am just going to sit here and listen.

Pride of Man: Me too. I am so tired but I wanted to hear what was going to be said. I know most of dad's thoughts; however I have never heard him lay out what he actually believes all at one time.

Man: First of all I am not running for any kind of office and second I do not know if I have everything figured out. I must remind everyone that our trust must be in Jesus Christ for He and He alone is going to be our answer.

Friend of Man: What do you think is the best kind of government, democracy, socialism, communism, or a dictatorship?

Man: Of course it is a democracy, but we are not a democracy we are a republic.

Pride of Man: What is the difference?

Man: In a true democracy the people all vote on every law that is passed and by a plurality of the votes the law is enacted. In a Republic we elect representatives to make our laws. Here in the United States we have three branches of government, the president or the executive branch who everyone thinks is in charge of the country, however he is not the only person in charge for he is subject to the congress. That consist of the Senate and House of Representatives who have the power to override any law that the president might try to impose on people. Now we also have the judiciary or Supreme Court that can rule a law as constitutional and prohibit it from becoming law. For a form of government, ours works fairly well however there seems to be one major problem with it.

Pride of Man: What is that?

Man: The influence of Lucifer on the government, not only ours but governments throughout the world. For governments consist of people who like us are not perfect but are born under the curse of Adam's sin.

Friend of Man: There you go again, talking about Lucifer or the devil or as you like to call him, the King Mosquito. Why do you call him that? I think you told me once but refresh my memory again. Please.

Man: Because he is always drawing the very lifeblood out of man and is one of the leading carriers of diseases. Also after he has bitten you he always leaves his mark on you to remind you that he has recently been in touch with you. His influence is affecting every person on the planet including the members in government, for government is made up of people and as he is influencing the people in government he can control our very own individual lives there by advancing his agenda.

Pride of Man: How do you think he accomplishes his goal of getting his agenda across?

Man: Simple, or maybe not so simple, for as I have noticed Lucifer in action over the years I see him as a very devious creature. You ask what his agenda is, I can tell you. His agenda is to get you so dependent on government that you will completely forget about God. He knows that Jesus said he will supply all of our needs according to his riches in glory. Notice that I said needs and not greed's. Now he usually does this through other people and if you are on the receiving end and someone helps you say financially or emotionally and they tell you that they felt inspired by God to help you then you are going to start thinking about the God that they serve. It is a form of evangelism. Saint Francis of Assisi said; "preach the gospel and when necessary use words!" Lucifer cannot have this. So one of the ways he works is to get you to depend on government rather than on God or God's people. For he knows that for you to have an encounter with God it is usually preceded by you having known a person who has a relationship with Him.

Friend of Man: I guess I would have to agree with that, for over the years the only time I feel like I have been in the presence of God or seen Him in action is when I am with the three of you.

Man: Thank you. Anytime you want us to pray for you let us know.

Friend of Man: Are you saying when it comes to government that you are opposed to all of it?

Man: No because of the fallen state that man is now in, without government we would be in utter chaos. Look at what you see going on now with government supposedly in control. Look at the number of murderers, rapes, child molestation, robberies, and the list could go on and on. Governments cannot control what is going on in the hearts of man. Even in the Old Testament they had set up captains of thousands, captains of hundreds, and captains of tens. We are commanded to pray for those who rule over us for God knows that we have to have laws to abide by. When they asked Jesus about paying taxes He replied with a question of whose image was on the coin. When they replied Caesars, he said render unto Caesar what is Caesars but to render unto God what is God's. So you see

God knows that we have to have laws to abide by, however it helps when our government leaders have a relationship with our Lord and honor Him. You can read in the Old Testament about the various kings. When the Israelites were doing well it was because the present king was serving God and when things were bad the king that was reigning at the time was usually allowing false idols to be erected.

Friend of Man: Do you think in heaven there will be a democratic form of government?

Man: No, absolutely not.

Friend of Man: Why not? You just said that our form of government works fairly well. I am like you, I have studied government for most of my adult life and I have never seen anything better than the one we have.

Man: I will answer that in a moment, however right now I want to tell you how this started. Israel for years had no king, God was their king. The people of Israel decided they wanted a king like the other nations so God granted them their wish and gave them a king. From then on various Kings ruled over them, some were good Kings and had compassion on the people and some were very harsh. During this period God kept promising them that a Messiah would come who would rule and He would be an Israelite like them. However when Jesus appeared on earth He did not come as a king but rather as a servant, who proclaimed that he who would be greatest of all, let him be servant of all. He also proclaimed that the meek would inherit the earth. Now when He returns He will return as the King of Kings, something we believers are highly anticipating. He will rule and reign on earth, for a thousand years along with we who believe in Him.

Friend of Man: Do you mean He will come and write a new constitution or something like that?

Man: No, for He said He would write His laws on our hearts and we will know His perfect will all the time. This is why it is so imperative to know Him and not just know about Him.

Friend of Man: How can you possibly know him like that?

Man: The Apostle Paul said that I might know Him and the power of His resurrection and the fellowship of His sufferings.

Friend of Man: What do you mean about the fellowship of his sufferings?

Pride of Man: Let me answer that. It is like this, when people go out and party together there is a fellowship or friendship that develops from doing and experiencing the same thing. When a group of people get together and are in the same line of work they immediately develop a special bond because they have been experiencing the same thing. The same applies to sports fans, music lovers, truck drivers, college professors, or people who love the Lord. When people experience the same thing there is a fellowship that develops. When we suffer with pain or even emotional distress our fellowship with our Lord is greatly increased because no one suffered any more than Him. Through it we have a lasting bond with Him that will endure throughout eternity. Remember He willingly laid His life down for us so that we could be united with God so our fellowship with Him could be restored as in the beginning. So our suffering is an opportunity to know him rather than to curse him. It is like the bible verse that says many are called but few are chosen, a verse that is greatly misunderstood by most believers. Suffering draws us to God and everyone will be given the opportunity or the calling to experience it in one form or another.

Friend of Man: I thought we were talking about government. How did we get on this subject?

Man: We were talking about God writing His laws on our heart and everyone would know Him and this is one of the most effective ways of knowing Him. But let us continue on the subject some more. When Jesus was tempted in the wilderness for forty days, Satan carried Him up and showed Him all the kingdoms of the world and proclaimed that if He would bow down and worship him that he would give Him all of them, for they were his and he could give them to whoever he chose. Think about that statement, they are his and he can give them to whoever he chooses. This does not mean that our God is not in control.

Friend of Man: It sounds like it does.

Man: No, it is God giving us that freedom of choice again, for He said choose you this day whom you will serve. Let's face it, mankind has done some marvelous things, we have built automobiles, highways to drive them on, increased food production, put people in space, and we could go on and on. But when we are all alone there is still that constant yearning that desires to be filled. God is the only one that can fill it. Lucifer comes along and substitutes what God has to offer by promising you more meaningless promises.

Friend of Man: Like what?

Man: It depends on what he thinks he can give you to keep you from seeking after God. With some it is lust, drugs, or in some it is having a sense of feeling more important than others, for instance as is the case of most movies stars. But with most people all he has to do is give them a sense of false security and just let them go on their merry way and not give them any reason to call on God. Unfortunately a lot of churches have fallen into this category. Luke warm is the terminology used in the scriptures and we know what the Lord thinks of that. Then he will place a certain number of people in high places in business and government and bombard us with thoughts of wishing we could be like them. For instance, do you remember that clown a few years ago who said he was going to give ten billion dollars to some world program to help the poor nations of the world? He announced it on TV and made the statement that it was contingent on the stock of his company doing well. Evidently God was not impressed because in less than a year his stock prices declined so much that he lost more than the ten billion dollars that he was going to give away. These are just various ways that Lucifer tries to influence man, nevertheless if we are truthful we would all like to have that kind of influence given to us. But it is probably the grace of God that keeps us from attaining that kind of wealth for if we had acquired it I am sure that the same trappings of that wealth and influence would keep us separated from God. For if we were in want of nothing there would be no need to ask for God's help or just the opposite would happen.

Friend of Man: And what would that be?

Man: We would think that we were a very special person in the sight of God because we had been so richly blessed and therefore we would be greatly deceived. It is just one more part of how Lucifer is planning to keep us from knowing God. Another plan is to make politicians so enamored with their own self that they will institute programs for people who will not work with food stamps, free housing, pay their electric bills, and give them free medical treatment. Now these all sound like great programs they have and for some that are down and out they are life sustaining, however the majority of the time it harms the cause of Christ. You see this is supposed to be the work of the church but as the church does not do its job, government takes over and the church declines in stature. This is why democracies fail, eventually the people will demand or vote more help from the government, after a while there is more revenue going out than is coming in and the nation goes broke. The same principle applies to all governments. This is why heaven will have an order of God's laws written on men's hearts

Friend of Man: His plans seem to be working well, but the problems I see is that we have to pay for all of these programs that are being implemented upon us.

Man: That is right, for believers and unbelievers are paying dearly. The country is trillions of dollars in debt; our money is a Federal Reserve note which is nothing more than an I.O.U. that is not backed by anything more than their word. The same people that have created the trillions in debt are giving us an I.O.U. How does that make you feel?

Friend of Man: Scary!

Man: Well it should. Let me tell you, it is not going to get any better but much worse, and I mean much worse. Jesus said a time is coming upon the earth like nothing the world has ever experienced before. Think of that, never has the earth experienced anything like what is getting ready to come upon it. Look at the past; we have had floods, droughts, earthquakes, fires, famines, and wars unimaginable. We can have all of these things happen at once along with a complete economic breakdown. Jesus said it would be so bad that even the very elect would not survive; whoever they are.

Friend of Man: But why would He let this happen?

Man: Because God loves us and he wants us to love Him and to know Him. The best way to get our attention is to bring hardship and suffering. He promised not to destroy the world by water again, however the next time it will be by fire, maybe not actual fire or maybe so. More than likely trials by fire like the three Hebrew children went through. God will stand in the midst of it with us for the whole system will end before His new kingdom is set up. Only during that time is it going to come on the whole earth rather than on certain individuals like in the case with the Pride of Man. Then we will realize that our trust in government which is backed by Lucifer will fail, and fail miserably, for it cannot and will not stand. That is when the new millennium will start; when man has God's laws written on their hearts. Then the Lord's Prayer will be fulfilled, "Thy kingdom come; Thy will be done; on earth as it is in heaven."

Chapter Twenty Nine

Man: Lord, it is 3:00 AM and I cannot sleep.

God: I love you Man.

Man: I love you too Lord.

God: Get some rest.

Chapter Thirty

Man: OK, I will be right there.

Pride of Man's Joy of Man: Look at him, he is turning so yellow and he is very lethargic. I did not know what to do, I am so glad you came right over. I have not slept in two days. I have been praying and worrying and I just can't take it anymore. I am so scared. What should we do?

Man: Is his sugar OK?

Pride of Man's Joy of Man: Yes, I have checked it and it is staying constant at the acceptable levels.

Man: We have to take him to the hospital for I am concerned about the yellow look that he has, it can only mean one thing.

Pride of Man's Joy of Man: Liver?

Man: Yes. Let's get him to the hospital.

Pride of Man: I feel so sick. Where are we going?

Pride of Man's Joy of Man: We are taking you to the hospital.

Pride of Man: Not again, I was just there five months ago. Oh, hi dad, I just recognized you. Do you think I should go to the hospital too?

Man: Yes son, you are turning yellow and we need to see what is wrong.

Pride of Man: I am so tired, let me just lay here in the back seat until we arrive.

Man: OK, get some rest and we will be praying.

Pride of Man's Joy of Man: God, please, please, let him be OK.

Man: Amen.

Chapter Thirty One

Great friend of God: I am so sorry to hear that, I will keep him in my prayers.

Man: Thank you. How are you doing, I know that you are almost unable to leave the house with the pain in your back. Is there any relief in sight?

Great friend of God: No the surgery was not any help, I think it might even have made it worse. How about Pride of Man's Joy of Man? How is she taking this news?

Man: She held out hope until the very last but when we saw the x-rays and it showed the cancer she was devastated. I love that girl beyond description.

Great friend of God: And you say they cannot do anything, chemo or surgery?

Man: No because of the cystic fibrosis he is so week that the chemo and radiation would kill him because the cancer is attached to his liver, intestines, his stomach, and pancreas. The doctors say a healthy person would only have a forty percent survival rate. It is a seven hour surgery and his lungs would not handle that long of a time under anesthesia so even surgery is not an option. They inserted a drainage tube that is attached to his liver and it is helping to reduce the yellow look but it is just another thing to add to his pain, not to mention the added burden of care that has been placed on his Joy of Man.

Great friend of God: What now?

Man: He is at home under hospice care. They are giving him morphine for the pain and he is trying to take as little as possible because he wants to retain as much consciousness as he can so he can have the capability to converse with us.

Great friend of God: Jesus, Jesus, Jesus. Did they give him a time frame?

Man: Thirty days. I am really worried about Pride of Man's Joy of Man. She is having a hard time accepting this and wondering why God has not healed him.

Great friend of God: The only thing that comes to my mind is the story of Jesus at the pool of Bethesda. Do you remember when the angel would come down and trouble the water? The first one who would step in would be made whole. There was a man who was there who could not move so someone always stepped in ahead of him. He said that he had no man to put him in the water so he was always too late. Anyway Jesus healed him but you notice that there was no record of him healing everyone there. I do not know why but I wish I could give you and her an answer. If I could I would ask for Pride of Man's healing along with my own healing. It is still a walk of faith, and like you I have seen God heal some and even experienced it myself on some other issues besides the pain in my back. How are you holding up?

Man: I am trying to stay calm but it is hard. The lord is with me but I still feel alone. I have known that this day was coming for forty years. You think that you are prepared but when it happens it is like you were caught off guard. I cannot ever recall feeling this helpless. Please pray that I can remain strong for the Pride of Man's Joy of Man and his brother also.

Great friend of God: How is he doing? We have been so focused on Pride of Man that we have not talked about him lately.

Man: Health wise he is doing great. He weighs about 170 pounds and he goes to the gym about three times a week. I can tell you that he is devastated by this latest news. The two of them have had a closeness from being shackled with the same affliction over the years. Since Joy of Man left about a year ago it has affected him along with the Pride of

Man. I explained to them that the divorce statistics for people who have children with cystic fibrosis is around eighty five percent. I think that the parents feel guilty for their children having the disease so it leaves a vulnerable area for Lucifer to attack and he has been relentless in doing so over the years. Pray for her for I know that she will be having an extremely hard time dealing with this.

Great friend of God: I will. How is Friend of Man doing with his neuropathy?

Man: He is in more pain than you can imagine. I don't think I told you that he was in the hospital.

Great friend of God: No you did not. What happened?

Man: He was taking a lot of pain pills along with morphine and he had a mild heart attack. He is doing better now but he is still in a lot of pain, so much so that the last time I saw him he had tears in his eyes.

Great friend of God: Is he still asking questions about the Lord?

Man: I guess I forgot to tell you that his daughter found the Lord and she finally got him to pray and ask Jesus in his heart. He calls me and thanks me all the time for telling him about the Lord over the years and now he sends me emails all the time about Jesus. Again, the faithfulness of God answering our many prayers for him over the years.

Great friend of God: God brings another one to Himself through pain and suffering.

Man: Yes and it is too bad that it has to be that way. I am in no physical pain but the pain that I endure is just as bad and brings the same reaction which is to make me call out to Him.

Chapter Thirty Two

Pride of Man: Hi dad. Thanks for bringing the milk shake over. Actually I should thank you for all the food you keep bringing me, KFC, the hamburgers, and pizza. I really do appreciate it, not only for me but for my Joy of Man. I'm concerned about her for she is losing a lot of weight.

Man: You know that she loves you very much.

Pride of Man: Yes. I can tell you that she is the best thing that has happened to me. Dad I am now an official drug addict. I have to keep increasing the morphine for the pain so if my mind wanders forgive me. When they diagnosed me they said that I only had thirty days but it is five months now. I am so grateful for the extra time to spend with her and you along with our Lord. By the way Great friend of God called me last week and said that she was going to send me an email about what I was going through. Here is a copy of it; you might want to read it when you get a chance. It is very informative. She has always been a saint to me and I am so grateful to have had her in my life.

Man: It is strange how the Lord sends someone into your life unexpectedly and they became a rock of encouragement over so many years. I cannot think of a better person to know and I thank God every day for her. I had better go for I can see you are tired. Get some rest.

Pride of Man: Thanks dad. I love you and if I should pass soon please keep the faith and I will see you on the other side.

Man: I love you too son, you will never know how much.

Chapter Thirty Three

Pride of Man's Joy of Man: It is 7:30 AM...Uh, well... You need to call me.

Man: I hope this is not what I fear it is.

Pride of Man's Joy of Man: I got up this morning and the first thing I did was check on him like I do every morning. I knew immediately. Can you come right over?

Man: I will be right there.

Pride of Man's Joy of Man: Look at him, he looks like he is asleep on the couch, doesn't he?

Man: He is asleep. Just think, he is breathing better now than he has his entire life while he was here on earth. Have you notified his mother and brother?

Pride of Man's Joy of Man: Yes, I also called hospice and they are sending a van to pick him up. Will you stay with me for a couple of days until my mother arrives? She is leaving now.

Man: Of course.

Chapter Thirty Four

Man: Your mother will be here tomorrow morning. Did you ever read the email that Great friend of God sent to Pride of Man a few months ago?

Pride of Man's Joy of Man: No.

Man: Here, let me a read it to you.

Great friend of God: Dearest Pride of Man. I think about and pray for you daily but more importantly our Lord cares about you and "His thoughts concerning you are more than the sands in the sea!!!" David cried out with these words... How precious also are thy thoughts unto me, O god! How great is the sum of them! If I should count them they are more in number than the sand: when I awake I am still with Thee; psalm 139: 17-18 KJV. When we love someone they are always on our mind. Our Lord proved his love for us on Calvary. God's love is selfless, not selfish as we well know, and how we praise Him for this great love for us all.

Then why this ongoing sufferings which you have endured for most of your life and why the added afflictions to your already burdened plight? Why the increased hardships these serious troubles have wrought in your life? This all reminds us of His life, Jesus, chosen and sent by the Father to temporarily lay aside His Kingly robes to become an obedient servant, the One who would become our Way, our Truth, and our very Life. He would have to endure the depths of mental and physical anguish and would suffer distresses, heartaches, and ultimately physical death for our redemption. Therefore, He who knew no sin, sickness, or death became sin for us that we might be set free from the bondage of corruption! Why did the Father choose this suffering, this ransom for our salvation? Was it His life; is that the price He would have to pay to liberate the captives we had become to sin, sickness, and death? God took all the suffering sins raging within men's souls and laid them on Jesus Christ, His son. His strategy to defeat the Evil One who deceptively led man into sin was God's love. He would take all our sufferings which led to death upon Himself! His suffering brought Him physical death so that our sufferings would result in eternal life. For Jesus said in John 11: 25-26 to Mary when her brother and His friend died; "I am the resurrection and the life, he that believeth in me though he were dead, yet shall he live, and whosoever liveth and believeth in me shall never die."

So through one man's disobedience (Adam) sin, sickness, and death fell upon us all that through another man's obedience (Jesus the Christ), we can inherit eternal life after physical death as a believer in Him. This is the knowledge of our ongoing existence after physical death; to be in our heavenly Father through His Son by the power of the Holy Spirit forever! This deals with the Evil One, Satan, or the King Mosquito, as your dad likes to call Him. He is the one who tempted man and continues to tempt men to accuse God and reject His love, leaving them to live in their own pride, the very cause of his own downfall from his heavenly position; pride was his downfall and is his chief weapon against those in Christ who are called God's sons.

Our Father's love suffered in Christ for our sake and showed that we might be set free in knowing, accepting, and believing these truths, for Jesus said "you shall know the truth and that truth shall set you free." John 8: 32 and if the Son shall make you free, you shall be free indeed. John 8: 36. You know this good news Pride of Man, and God's answer to our question, why must we bear such awful sufferings? It was not like this in the beginning, there was no sin, sickness, or death until man usurped his will over God's will. Before this he enjoyed a continued experience of life, fellowship, and contentment with his creator. The serpent's prideful lies brought their bondage and separation from the Fathers love. Adam was the son of God, Luke 3: 38, "which was the son of Enos, which was the son of Seth, which was the son of Adam, which was the son of God."

Pain and suffering are an equalizer, bringing things into balance, for it gets our attention, causes us to think, helps us to discern good and evil. We are then set free, humbled and filled with the joy of knowing that our heavenly Father never causes our sufferings, rather uses what the enemy meant for harm by turning it around and working it out for our good in the end.

Here are some scriptures to consider.

Romans 8: 28-39 KJV

28 And we know that all things work together for good for them that love God who are called according to His purpose.

29 For whom He did foreknow, He also did predestinate to be conformed to the image of His Son that He might be the firstborn among many brethren.

30 Moreover whom He did predestinate, them He also called: and whom He called, them He also justified; and whom He justified, them He also glorified.

31 What shall we say to these things? If God be for us, who can be against us?

32 He that spared not His own Son, but delivered Him up for us all, how shall He not with Him also freely give us all things?

33 Who shall lay anything to the charge of God's elect? It is God that justifieth.

34 Who is he that condemneth? It is Christ that died, yea rather, that is risen again, who is even at the right hand of God, who also maketh intercession for us.

35 Who shall separate us from the love of Christ? Shall tribulation, or distress or persecution, or famine, or nakedness, or peril, or sword?

36 As it is written, for thy sake we are killed all day long, we are accounted as sheep for the slaughter.

37 Nay, in all these things we are more than conquerors through Him that loved us.

38 For I am persuaded, that neither death, nor life, nor angles, nor principalities, nor powers, nor things present, nor things to come,

39 Nor height, nor depth, nor any other creature, shall be able to separate us from the love of God, which is in Christ Jesus our Lord.

This is why suffering is allowed to still manifest and wreak havoc in our daily lives. So then remember what St. Paul wrote in romans 8: 16- 18.

16 The Spirit itself beareth witness with our spirit, that we are the children of God:

17 And if children, then heirs; heirs of God. And joint heirs with Christ; if so be that we suffer with Him, that we may be also glorified together.

18 For I reckon that the sufferings of this present time are not worthy to be compared with the Glory which shall be revealed in us.

This is where some are in the realm of suffering Pride of Man, for you are currently fighting the battle for your physical life. Longsuffering seems so cruel and as in your case has gone on for years. Few have consistently suffered as you have for so long a time and now adding insult to injury you have been hit with another blow. You patiently endure being a strong witness to all who know you; I am currently on that list.

This would have taken anyone else down and out, but not you Pride of Man, not you. And why is that? Years ago you had questions about the disease you later found out you and your younger brother were born with, questions as to how a loving God could allow such suffering. Here again we found Pride of Man concerned for his brother rather than for himself. What a lesson you taught those who know you about the love of God. God, and only God, who has graced you with his strength through these times could have given you such peace in the midst of your many raging storms. This He has given you for you have a soft heart, a gentle teachable spirit, because you are His! In all these years of suffering you continue to be a testimony and a faith builder to others, giving hope in the midst of their own trials. Because you have turned to Him in your sufferings you have encouraged others, giving them hope and causing them to have faith in the times of their own afflictions and troubles. Thank you again dear brother, your life is an encouragement in Christ to many others.

You are in our thoughts and prayers daily, we bless you Pride of Man and the Lord's purpose for your life as you continue to be that beacon of light which reflects His life that we all so desperately need. Saint Francis of Assisi said, "Preach the gospel and when necessary use words!" Your life is a testimony to this brother Pride of Man.

With love, Sister Great Friend of God.

P.S. Thought the following would bless you.

The prayer of St. Francis:

Lord, make me an instrument of your peace;

Where there is hatred, let me sow love;

Where there is injury, pardon;

Where there is doubt, faith;

Where there is despair; hope;

Where there is darkness' light;

Where there is sadness, joy;

O divine master; grant that I may so much not seek to be consoled as to console;

To be understood as to understand;

To be loved as to love.

For it is in giving that we receive;

It is in pardoning that we are pardoned;

And it is in dying that we are born to eternal life.

St. Francis was born at Assisi in 1182. After a care free youth, he turned his back on inherited wealth and committed himself to God. Like many early saints, he lived a very simple life of poverty, and in doing so, gained a reputation of being a friend of animals. He established the rule of St. Francis, or the Franciscans. He died in 1226 at the age of 44.

The prayer has many of the biblical truths of what it means to be a Christian, to seek to give, and in so doing, receive blessings, that the Lord's Prayer to ask God to forgive us as we forgive, and that the goal of eternal life can only result from us putting to death our own sinful lives.

Pointers of prayer:

Sometimes Christians are called to turn the world upside down. To bring the exact opposite of what we find in our world. St. Francis's prayer is a bold one, asking for strength to give of ourselves to meet the needs of others. He recognizes that it is in giving that we receive, that as we give of ourselves we receive the peace and blessing of our risen Lord Jesus. We cannot earn eternal life, but we are pardoned from the sins that block our claim to it.

Think about the situations that you are involved in that require peace, consolation, hope, light, and joy.

Then if you are bold enough, pray the prayer!

.

God, the Mosquito, and Man

Friend of Man	Jimmy
Great friend of God	Sister Nita
Brother of Man	Ron
Joy of Man	Joy
Pride of Mans Joy of Man	Kim
Pride of Man	Tim
Man	Yours Truly

God, the Mosquito, and Man

Special thanks to Brian for the help and encouragement in telling this story.

God Bless You Brother!

God, the Mosquito, and Man

16282919R00134

Made in the USA
Charleston, SC
13 December 2012